Home *work* Improvement

Roberta Schneiderman with Stephen Werby

An Imprint of ScottForesman
A Division of HarperCollinsPublishers

GoodYearBooks

are available for preschool through grade 6 for every basic curriculum subject plus many enrichment areas. For more GoodYearBooks, contact your local bookseller or educational dealer. For a complete catalog with information about other GoodYearBooks, please write:

GoodYearBooks

Scott, Foresman and Company
1900 East Lake Avenue
Glenview, IL 60025

Book design and illustration by Amy O'Brien Krupp.
Copyright © 1996 Roberta Schneiderman with Stephen Werby.
All Rights Reserved.
Printed in the United States of America.

ISBN 0-673-36309-0

1 2 3 4 5 6 7 8 9 - MH - 03 02 01 00 99 98 97 96 95

Only portions of this book intended for classroom use may be reproduced without permission in writing from the publisher.

Preface

I have worked as an educator for over 20 years. That work has brought me into direct and continuous contact with students, teachers, and parents. As a result of my work, I am convinced that we must begin to discuss learning habits as soon as possible in a child's schooling. In the early school years, most children and parents are enthused about learning. Unfortunately, many parents don't realize the value of the skills and knowledge that they can share with their children at this time.

Homework Improvement empowers you—the parents of children grades 4 through 8—to support your children's education. This book provides the tools you need to develop learning habits in your children that will see them through their years of schooling and beyond. With efficient learning habits, your children will maximize their potential whether they are average learners, gifted students, or even if they have diagnosed learning difficulties. An early start on good learning habits will give them an early start on success.

Roberta Schneiderman

Contents

Introduction

Parent Power 1
    Early Involvement in Your Child's Learning 1
    What the Experts Say 2
What Will Help Children Most? 3
    Throw Away Your Assumptions 3
    Getting Children Organized 4
    Planning to Remember 4
    Efficient Studying 5
How *Homework Improvement* Can Help You 7

1 The Organization Tools 9

The Daily Assignment Planner 10
    Activities for Younger Children 13
    Activities for Older Children 15
The Monthly Calendar 16
    Activities for Younger Children 16
The Weekly Schedule 18
    Activities for Younger Children 19

2 The Reading Tools 21

Read It and Own It 22
The Story Analyzer 27
    Additional Applications 30
    Activities for Younger Children 30

3 The Practice Tools 33

Flash Cards 34
Matching Deck 36
Sorting Boxes 38
    Activities for Younger Children 39
Split Sheets 39
Four-Column Pages 42
    Activities for Younger Children 46
Puzzle Charts 47
    Activities for Younger Children 48

4 The Writing Tools 51

Writing Organizer 53
Library Paper Builder 55
    Activities for Younger Children 59

5 The Analysis Tools — 61

Problem and Reason Analyzer — 63
    Activities for Younger Children — 65
Test Analysis Form — 65

6 Add Your Own Tools — 67

Mnemonics — 68
    Activities for Younger Children — 71
Colors — 72
Papers, Pens, and Pencils — 73
Colored Pens and Highlighters — 74
Word Associations — 74
Corrected Homework — 77
Guess the Test — 78
Sneak-a-Peek Sheets — 79
The Testing Issue — 80
Music, Music, Music — 83
Tape Recorder Magic — 84
Taking Words/Getting Questions — 84

7 The End and the Beginning — 89

Appendix — 93

Footnotes — 117

Introduction

Parent Power

As the parent of a child in grades four through eight, you possess monumental power. You have the power to change the course of your child's education and thereby change the course of her life. Parent Power is more than just becoming involved in your child's schooling. It may be the deciding factor in your child's success and, therefore, in her future.

Homework Improvement gives you all the Parent Power necessary to direct your child toward success. This book will help you gently guide your child to approach schoolwork correctly, complete assignments, learn more, and learn faster. You will have the confidence that the help you're giving is the right kind of help. You will know that every suggestion encourages your child on the road to independent lifelong learning. Every idea and tool in *Homework Improvement* will help your child to learn in school today and face tomorrow's challenges.

Early Involvement in Your Child's Learning

If you wait until the high school years to get involved in your child's learning, you've waited too long. Many of today's high school parents are unable to help their teenagers because teens state in no uncertain terms that they don't want help. At that point, you're not credible and you can't open the door to learning. But you can do it when your child is younger.

Children in grades four to eight are more likely to welcome your input. Once you've become involved at an early age, you will have opened the lines of communication. You won't have to deal with many of the problems that parents of high schoolers often face. You will have built for your child a foundation in learning that she will use naturally in her high school years.

What evidence indicates the inadvisability of waiting until the high school years? Consider whether or not the following observations might describe you in a few years.

◆ High school parents say they are tired, especially if their children have experienced years of difficulty in school. Many feel that they have been fighting a losing battle, and that there is nothing more they can do. In spite of years of attempting to help, the problems just keep getting worse. Many say they really don't know how to help and never did.

Homework Improvement

- High school students think that parents don't know anything about how things are taught in school today, and they certainly don't want their parents' help.
- Students who have spent nine or ten years working one way, whether or not that way is efficient, often view new methods as "dumb." Their negative attitudes block any potential for improvement.

As parents of fourth- through eighth-graders, you have an advantage because younger children are more apt to talk about school and perhaps ask for help in studying. Daily dialogues about school allow you to know "how things are being taught in school today." Once you stimulate the dialogue, it is easy to move from "what happened during the day" to the assignments and tasks required of your child and how they will be accomplished. Younger children are less likely to be closed-minded about trying new ways of learning. If you are active in keeping your child open to new ideas about learning, then you and the school will have a much better chance of correcting problems if they occur.

What the Experts Say

Research says that parental involvement makes a difference in the school achievements of children. Consider these findings.

From *A Handbook on Home-School Collaboration*, published by the Massachusetts State Department of Education:

> "Neither the school alone nor the parents alone will be able to deal with the complex issues facing children today." [1]

> "This notion of the family as educator is not new. What is new is the growing understanding that the responsibility for children's school performance must be a shared responsibility." [2]

From findings of a survey of 25,000 American eighth graders, their parents, teachers, and principals, by the Office of Educational Research and Improvement in Washington, D.C.:

> "Achievement of not only our national goals but also state and community education goals will not happen without significantly more parental involvement." [3]

> "If we want children to have high expectations about learning, then all of us—especially parents—must regularly send those signals." [4]

> "We cannot expect others to perform those duties and we cannot expect children to do well without the guidance, the tutoring, the nurturing, and the commitment of parents." [5]

From an Oregon school study:

> "Academic involvement (by parents) not only produces academic improvement, but also leads to a more positive attitude toward school by the students. This

improvement occurs without regard to socioeconomic status or educational achievement of the parents." [6]

Suzanne Ziegler, writing for the Research Services of the Toronto Board of Education on "The Effects of Parent Involvement on Children's Achievement," found that:

> "[T]he gap so frequently found between working class children and middle class children is explained, in substantial part, by certain differing patterns of child-parent and parent-school interaction." [7]

> She also found that parents can be taught "to be as effective as some parents already are." [8]

> "The children of parents who are aware of what their offspring are studying at school and who are in regular communication with their teachers continue to show higher school achievement than others, all the way through secondary school." [9]

> According to her research, "The evidence suggests that no other single focus has the potential to be as productive for students as the closer linking of home and school, of parents and teachers." [10] And finally she states that "research findings accumulated over two decades . . . show that children have an advantage in school when their parents encourage and support their school activities." [11]

In *Strong Families, Strong Schools,* published by the U.S. Department of Education, the importance of parental involvement continues to be emphasized:

> "Families need to be involved in improving learning in the home and in every school across this nation if our children are to become competent scholars and more successful and productive citizens." [12]

What Will Help Children Most?

Throw Away Your Assumptions

When you engage the various tools of *Homework Improvement,* you may have to suspend some of your assumptions about how your children do their schoolwork.

Assumption 1: *The word* studying *means something to your child.* When your child is told to study for Friday's test, does she know what that means? Many children *think* they know, but they really don't. Too many students think that staring at a book is studying. Study skills are not inborn. If you assume that your child knows how to

study simply because she knows how to read, you're compounding the problem for later schooling. These skills need to be taught, and your child needs to learn them.

Assumption 2: *A child has a repertoire of ways to approach academic demands, so when given an assignment, she decides what is required before settling on the best method for completing the assignment.* It's just not true. Most kids can't name a single studying tool other than flash cards, let alone an entire repertoire.

You may be making other assumptions about how your child approaches schoolwork. Discard all of them. Instead, start by assuming that your child does not possess adequate learning skills. Then you can start her on the right path. Using the various tools and ideas in *Homework Improvement* makes learning fun and easy. Your child's self-esteem will grow as success builds upon success.

Getting Children Organized

Children can find countless obstacles, both real and imagined, to prevent them from doing schoolwork successfully. Here are some of them:

I forgot my books!

I forgot the page!

It's a dumb assignment and the teacher is dumb!

I'm dumb! I can't do it! I don't understand!

I don't remember what to do!

I don't have anything to do!

Studying doesn't work, it doesn't help me!

Does this sound familiar? It does to too many parents, but the real dilemma is what to do about the obstacles. At the fourth- to eighth-grade level, you can do a great deal!

Planning to Remember

The demands made on parents are overwhelming: a first (and sometimes a second) job; evening community meetings; attendance at the fitness center; time to shop, cook, clean; and taxiing children around town to scouts, pee-wee football, gymnastics, or appointments. If you don't keep an orderly calendar, you can't remember where you are expected to be.

You, as a parent, must help your child think about her calendar, her schedule. *At least 50 percent of the reason for lack of success in school can be attributed to an absence of organization.* Take the simple idea of remembering to do one's homework, or remembering to do it but not leaving enough time to do it. For example, if a spelling test is planned on Friday and a dentist appointment and gymnastics meet are on Thursday, then Thursday is probably not the most efficient time to study. Studying should be planned for Tuesday and Wednesday with a ten-minute review on Thursday night. Once your child understands that time is a limited commodity, she will understand the value of organization.

You can even teach younger children that time can only be spent once. If playtime is too long, then TV time will need to be shorter, for example. The idea is to make the child understand that planning her time will allow her to do everything.

This is your opportunity to teach her about organization and its relationship to responsibility. Preadolescents always want to act older, and it is your job both to encourage that personal growth and to prevent behaviors that you deem inappropriate. Encourage your child to take charge of her schedule. Tell her that the more responsibility she assumes successfully, the more you will give her, and that completing responsibilities will demonstrate to you that she truly is "big enough" to do some of the things for which she continually asks permission.

To help her along this path, draw parallels between the assignment notebooks used by students and the shopping lists and sophisticated business diaries used by adults. Your fourth- to eighth-grader wants to act beyond her years. Convince her that being organized enough to remember responsibilities is the most grown-up thing she can do. Once you introduce the idea of organization to your child, you, the parent, must support its value and assist in its continued use as educational demands increase. *Children don't forget to do their assignments. They simply don't plan to remember them.*

Instilling the idea of organizational responsibilities at an early age can result in a gradual, natural transition to complete and well-organized school lives for adolescents. Assignment notebooks need to be maintained in a systematic and organized fashion. *Parents who help their children to establish and maintain an organized assignment notebook will reap the later benefits as calm supportive parents of achieving adolescents.*

Homework Improvement shows you how to construct and use tools that will help your child learn to organize her schoolwork and subsequently her life.

Efficient Studying

Now that your child is organized, she is on her way to efficient studying. The word *studying* could be the most interesting word in education: it means so much to teachers and so little to students. Many students don't really know the meaning of the word *study*, but they understand *homework:* they write something. It's not difficult, therefore, to understand why the most common definition of *studying* is "I just read it over and over."

Reading and rereading works for some children, but only those who have high powers of concentration, a good memory, and a dedicated sense of purpose. These kids, the exceptions to the rule, are highly organized naturally. For too many children, that method of studying will result in poor grades and discouragement about the merits of studying. If that's your child's only method, her difficulties will begin as school demands increase.

Children whose only study method is to read and reread material often sit down (or more frequently, lie down) and, with a book in hand and radio set to a favorite station, they begin studying. They read a few sentences, think about something else, try to read a few

Homework Improvement

more sentences, look at the clock and think, "About fifteen more minutes should do it." Meanwhile, they begin to yawn and wonder why they feel so tired. Here's the message the brain is getting: "No physical movement other than eyes moving across the page . . . mind wandering . . . must be getting time to shut down here . . . not much happening." Of course they claim that studying doesn't help! The truth is that *their* studying didn't help. They didn't know *how to study*.

Efficient studying requires the use of more than just eyes. Complete studying should involve several senses and employ a variety of tools. Mere reading and rereading does not work as efficient studying for most children because it is incomplete.

Even if your child's dominant learning style is visual (that is, she learns best by using her eyes and she likes to study by reading material over and over again), she needs to learn to adapt her learning style to the demands of the task. When that task involves studying for any kind of demonstration of knowledge—a quiz or test, a presentation in front of the class, or any demonstration that she has acquired the knowledge she was supposed to acquire—the study method should approximate what she actually will be doing in the evaluation.

For example, if she is studying for a written spelling test, the final step in studying needs to be a practice test where she writes the words. If she is studying for a spelling bee, the final step should be oral, not written. An oral practice quiz will help for an oral test, but will likely result in a poorer grade if the test is written.

Let's examine why oral quizzing may be a problem. You pronounce the word; your child hesitates. You pronounce it again and unconsciously emphasize the difficult syllable, or perhaps raise your eyebrows when she spells the word with an *a* instead of an *o*. Your child immediately self-corrects, saying, "I meant an *o*." Satisfied that she knows the word, you praise and go on to the next word. At the end of this process, you and your child are satisfied and hope for the best on Friday's spelling test.

During Friday's test, your child is asked to fill in the blanks in sentences using the spelling words. She must both remember and spell the words. Your child stumbles over the spelling; you're not there to emphasize the difficult portion of the word or to raise your eyebrows to signal that she needs the *o*, not the *a*. After she receives a poor score on the test, she gives the studying process negative press. "Why study, it doesn't help!" "I'm dumb!" "The test is dumb!" "You saw it, Mom and Dad, I got it right when I did it with you!"

Well, actually, that last point is correct. Your child did well when you studied together. So what went wrong? The answer is *nothing* because she knew the words at that time, and the answer is *everything* because she failed the test.

This is not really contradictory. Your child needed better information about the test format so that she could match her studying to it. The assignment that your child understood had no bearing on how she should study. She heard, "There will be a test on these words this Friday." All she knew was that she needed to study those words.

Using *Homework Improvement,* you will help your child understand that tests can take different forms and that studying must also take different forms. Your child will learn to ask for more information. Your child will learn that the more she knows about the test, the more efficient and productive her studying process will be. Conversely, the less she knows about the test, the less efficient and productive her studying process will be.

This is not to say that you should never quiz your child. Instead, the study method must make sense for the task required during the test or quiz. Using appropriate study methods means fewer surprises at test time. When the student studies what the teacher will be evaluating and, most importantly, in the same format as the method of evaluation, her grades soar!

Homework Improvement suggests a variety of study methods. Using many techniques teaches flexibility and results in a willingness to listen and follow through on the teacher's suggestions. *Homework Improvement* will awaken your child to the analysis and solution of learning problems.

How *Homework Improvement* Can Help You

Homework Improvement allows you to work as a facilitator with your child—a guide—in her learning. As soon as you begin to apply the methods in this book, you will both see immediate rewards in improved grades and a more positive attitude toward school. Later rewards will include your child's ability to solve problems because she will be able to *think* about how to solve a problem. She will no longer see difficult tasks as impossible, or view them with anger, fear, or indifference. Learning new material will now become a puzzle that both of you can solve easily:

"How can I best learn this?"

"What other methods can I use?"

"What can I do?"

The *I* in all of these statements means that your child understands the learning process and understands that she is responsible for her own education—not you, not the school, not

Homework Improvement

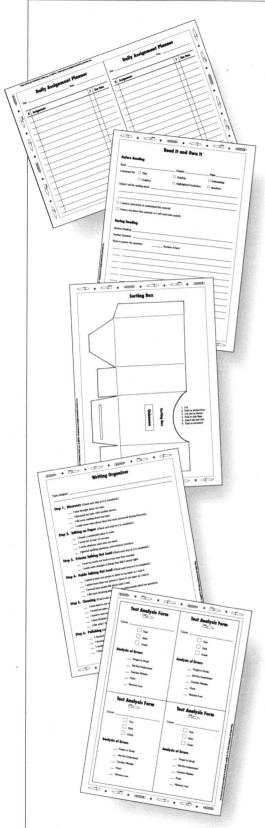

even the teacher. Research has proven that learning cannot take place if your child is not taking the responsibility to be an active learner. *Homework Improvement* provides the methods and tools for you, the facilitator, to help her become one.

The right tools make work easier. It is more difficult to turn a bolt with your fingers than with a tool designed for that purpose—a wrench, for example. In the same way, learning is made easier if you use the right tools—those found in *Homework Improvement*.

Homework Improvement offers five tools, each of which has several parts—the individual ways that each child learns how to learn. As each tool is used, your child's learning becomes easier and easier. The best part is that you don't have to start with all five tools. When you use *Homework Improvement,* you can start slowly! (In fact, you *should* start slowly.) Begin with one tool—any tool you choose. Then when that one is working, start another. When all five tools are working, the philosophy behind *Homework Improvement* is fully engaged, and your child is learning with maximum efficiency and speed!

You need not introduce the various tools in any order. It is helpful, however, to read about them in Chapters 1 to 5 in the order in which they are presented. Your child's needs should determine the order of introduction. Use the *Learning Habits Checklist* in the Appendix to determine areas that need focus.

You'll find *Activities for Younger Children* throughout the book to help students in grades one to three begin to acquire the habits they will need for school. All children, however, should be instructed in the use of the *Daily Assignment Planner* and the calendars. Organization is the driving force behind *Homework Improvement;* without a thorough understanding of the organizational tools, the benefits of the other tools will be limited.

The Organization Tools

Chapter 1

The Organization Tools

An organized student holds one of the most important keys to school success. The Organization Tool will provide the means to make learning efficient.

You, the parent, can identify with the value of organization. Jobs, family activities, and responsibilities in your community and neighborhood make tremendous demands on you. If you don't keep track of your responsibilities and activities, you're likely to miss one or two. And that can be stressful, not to mention embarrassing at times.

Lack of planning produces stress in your child as well, which results in failures at school. This causes tension, short tempers, anger, and frustration. Most importantly, these conditions sidetrack your child's learning. If your child is not organized, learning becomes inefficient, incomplete, and a chore.

Organization is necessary to your child's success. You must help him to think about his schedule; it's just as important as yours. As your child learns to *organize responsibilities,* he will create the right environment in which to learn.

The Organization Tool provides planning forms and suggestions, tools to help your child create an efficient assignment planner. Each tool will accelerate the learning process. Together, they will propel your child toward learning efficiently.

The Daily Assignment Planner

The *Daily Assignment Planner* will instill the habit of keeping a well-organized and accurate record of "Things To Do." While commercial assignment notebooks have been available for some time, their use in an integrated learning system has been under-recognized. Planning to remember assignments at an early age can evolve into keeping well-organized planning calendars that will be necessary as the demands of learning increase.

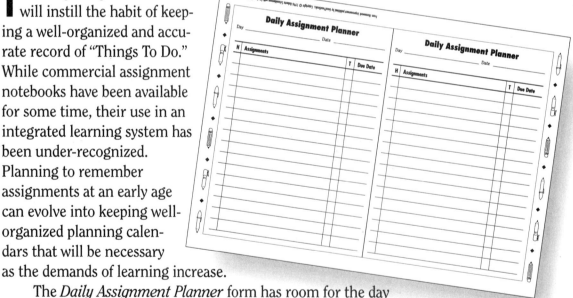

The *Daily Assignment Planner* form has room for the day and date at the top of the page and two writing columns in the body of the page: one for the details of the assignments and the other for the due dates so that your child has all the necessary information in one spot. You will notice two special columns on the *Daily Assignment Planner* page: an *H* column and a *T* column. The *H* column stands for *Help* and the *T* stands for "spend more *Time* with." The check-off format of these columns permits easy notation of additional needs on some assignments. The use of the two columns will be

discussed later in this chapter. Your child should use a new page for each day, an important concept to communicate logical divisions of time.

You will find a blank *Daily Assignment Planner* in the *Appendix*. To get your child started, copy enough forms for a month and assemble them into a three-ring binder. If you have a computer, you can create your own *Daily Assignment Planner*. Even better, have your child create the planner on the computer if you feel that he is capable. Just remember to include all the necessary parts: a new page for each day, room for today's date, and the details of the assignments. Parents who do not have access to either a copier or a computer can achieve the same results by helping their children to organize any small notebook with these components.

You should check this book daily. Discuss the school day generally with your child, as well as his specific notations. Use the planner as a starting point for your discussion of the day and to determine the extent of your child's success. Check the following:

◆ Make sure he has entered a notation for each subject or course that he had that day. If a particular area did not have an assignment, simply instruct him to write the word *none*. Explain that this will save him from worrying about whether he missed hearing the assignment or there really was none.

◆ Make sure that assignments are being completed. Communicating to the teacher any problem in this area will allow all three of you to work out a plan that will

The Organization Tools

enable you to know what work must be completed each night. School problems arise here first, but they can often be easily corrected if the parent and the teacher work together.

If there are no notations of assignments, discuss the day and help your child try to think of assignments that could have been listed. Stress that assignments are not just written things, but *thinking things* too! Explain to your child that thinking things are tasks done in school that seemed difficult or confusing, or topics that might be fun to explore. Explain that they should be listed in the *Daily Assignment Planner* to think about at home. Encourage the listing of these "self generated" assignments. This is a key to later success: studying, practicing, getting help on "hard stuff," and pursuing interests.

You should encourage notations that communicate your child's reaction to the class, course, or topic, as well as the assignment itself. Following are examples of specific situations in which this type of notation is useful:

◆ If there is to be further exploration, discussion, or work on a particular topic the next day, and your child doesn't really understand what has already been accomplished, ask him to check the *H* on the *Daily Assignment Planner* page. The word *Help* should be sufficient to alert you to a problem and to allow both of you to discuss a possible solution. (See *The Problem and Reason Analyzer,* Chapter 5, for specific ways to explore a problem.)

◆ The class explored, discussed, or worked on a particular topic that your child really enjoyed. Ask him to make a note about the topic in his *Daily Assignment Planner* and to check the *T* (for spend more *Time* on) so the two of you can discuss how he might further explore that topic. The *T* check should be sufficient to alert you to this interest. Discussions about what he found interesting should suggest how you could assist him in pursuing this topic. If you and your child are unable to think of ways to continue exploration of this topic, call the school and discuss it with the teacher. The teacher will be delighted to learn of this interest and may be very helpful in suggesting ways to do so.

For tasks not due the next day, help your child to separate the assignment into several parts; then help him list each part on successive days with appropriate due dates.

Sometimes assignments will have no due dates or will have a due date that is far into the future. Remember that an assignment without a due date encourages noncompletion.

Make it a point to discuss any assignment with a due date beyond "tomorrow," or for which the teacher has not yet designated a specific due date. Frequently, students think that they have unlimited time to address assignments with long time frames. As a result, they neglect the assignment completely because they forget about it or, even if they remember it, they don't have enough time to complete it.

In both cases you can help by discussing such assignments with your child. If a specific date does not materialize, then you and your child should outline steps to complete the assignment and arbitrarily assign dates that will allow him to finish before an assumed due date. Track these steps to completion the same way you've tracked other assignments by having your child enter them on specific days in his *Daily Assignment Planner*.

Be excited about what your child lists. Use the listings (or even a lack of listings) as a springboard for discussing school: your child's successful areas that day and your child's problem areas for the day. Remember that the purpose of working on assignment notebooks is to encourage and reinforce good organizational habits.

As he completes assignments, praise your child, and with much flourish, neatly cross them out. Any assignments not completed should be copied to the next day's list. Do not tear out any pages. They make a handy reference when reviewing for tests.

Use the second page of the *Daily Assignment Planner* to list any quiz or test grades, with your child present as you do so. This is a handy reference during meetings with teachers. Encourage and help your child to follow his status. Conferences and report cards are less likely to hold surprises and bad news if he crosses out completed assignments, lists quiz and test grades, and uses the planner to generate daily conversations with you about school. You will know how your child is doing on a daily basis.

Remember, small problems are the easiest to solve. The *Daily Assignment Planner* provides more than just a memory device for your child. It also alerts you immediately when problems arise. A phone call to the teacher following a low quiz grade, when your child completed all of the assignments that preceded it, can result in immediate assistance for your child. You can call attention to a problem before the teacher has an opportunity to address it, or even before the teacher is aware of it. If your community, like many, is experiencing increases in class sizes, your involvement will be even more important to your child's success.

Activities for Younger Children

Younger children receive far fewer homework assignments than do older children. Just because your child has only a few assignments does not mean that your child is too young to begin keeping an assignment notebook. There are many activities that you can do with a first- to third-grader that will provide incentive for daily use of an assignment notebook.

The key for these younger children is to get them into the habit of using a *Daily Assignment Planner*. Ask to see your child's planner each day and discuss any sketches or words he has added that day. The detail is less important for children in the first through third grades—a sketch or one or two words in the *Daily Assignment Planner* is sufficient to jog his memory when you discuss it at home. Any notations can be used as a springboard to talk about "what happened in school today." This not only establishes good lines of communication with your child, it also provides another reason for young children to keep the planner.

As your child gives you additional information during the discussion, write that information in the planner in the columns for assignment and due date. Children of this age who keep a *Daily Assignment Planner* will be very proud of it.

Positive reinforcement will go a long way toward continuing this important habit, so remember to praise your child whenever he has entered a sketch or words that suggest his assignment. Help him boast to relatives, grandparents, and other children about keeping the planner. Younger children want to be like the "big kids," and your praise and pride will reinforce a positive and necessary study habit.

Here are some ideas that will encourage the daily use of the planner, but you will be able to think of many more.

- ◆ Ask your child questions that can only be answered in school. Ask him to put his questions and their answers in his planner. Pose the questions at an opportune time (maybe at dinner) and present them as a game. Some examples follow, but specific questions that you have designed will be most meaningful and you will have fun thinking of them.

    How many kids were in class today?

    How many boys wore T-shirts with sports logos, and how many wore T-shirts with rock group logos?

    How many girls have long hair?

    How many boys have long hair?

    How many kids wore dark pants, and how many wore light pants?

Ask your child to find the answer the following day and write it next to the question in the *Daily Assignment Planner*. You can make this even more fun by having other family members guess the answers. Then the *Daily Assignment Planner* becomes the authority for judging who was closest.

This activity will not only reinforce the daily use of a planner, it will also raise your child's self-esteem as everyone looks to him as the "authority."

- ◆ Ask your child to copy something of interest from a book or the chalkboard every day for the two of you to discuss. This may be as simple as a word or two, or a sketch. You will be surprised how much you will have to discuss and how easily you can ingrain the habit of carrying and making notations in the planner.

- ◆ Create a series of questions and activities and number them. Perhaps you could think of twenty-five. Each

evening or morning, select three or four and challenge your child to find the answers that day and to write them in his planner. Some examples:

Find an item in the classroom that is smooth. Draw it in the planner.

Find something that is round and write the name of it in your planner.

Find something that starts with the letter *C*.

Find something that starts with *St*.

Find something that comes in pairs.

The possibilities are endless. The goal is to reinforce taking the *Daily Assignment Planner* to school every day and using it every day. Creating a purpose—in the form of a "seek and find" game—will encourage your child at an impressionable age even though the need to do so is not substantial. As he advances through school, the need to use parent-created questions and activities will decrease. You will, however, have established the proper habit.

Activities for Older Children

Children who are more advanced in their school needs begin to receive more assignments—from several times a week to daily. The following parent-directed activities will provide reinforcement for the correct usage of the *Daily Assignment Planner*.

- ◆ Create a point system with a reward. Each time you see that an assignment is correctly entered (date, details, due date, etc.) your child earns points towards a goal: staying up later on the weekend, watching a special TV show, etc. The points required to reach the goal should be more than could be received from just 1 or 2 correct entries. For example, 5 points required for the TV program, 10 required for a sleep-over, etc.

- ◆ If your child has difficulty in writing the full details of tasks, then create a system where bonus points are rewarded for correct assignment notation, as approved by the teacher. You could even use prizes, in addition to points—new T-shirts, special sneakers, etc.—if paying attention to details of assignments results in better grades. Rewards are thus provided for long-term accomplishment as well as short-term goals.

- ◆ A child who has some difficulty remembering to bring things home—a math book, a graded test paper, etc.—could receive bonus points for writing a reminder in his planner and following through on that notation. In this way, he is using the planner as a reminder for in-school activities as well as for home activities. It turns the planner into a Planner/Organizer—the same concept used by successful adults!

> The Organization Tools

The Monthly Calendar

Organization means not only remembering what has to be done for school; it also means planning for all the events in children's lives. Although it may not seem necessary for young children to plan ahead, development of this ability cannot start early enough. A child who grows up with a *Monthly Calendar* will continue to use one as life's demands increase.

Everything in your child's life is related to events in the lives of other family members and to activities with friends. A *Monthly Calendar* is an organizational tool that will help your child plan ahead and avoid conflicts. (Young children haven't yet learned how to handle conflicting demands on their time.)

The *Monthly Calendar* form provided in the *Appendix* has room for noting the month, dates, and events. This allows you and your child—and then your child alone—to visualize time commitments.

Display the *Monthly Calendar* in a prominent place for everyone in the family to see. This demonstration of its importance will encourage your child to use it. If several children in your family need to become proficient in using the calendar, be just as proud of all of them as they use it. Your pride in the older ones' usage will encourage the younger ones, too.

Enter everything that affects your child's schedule—appointments, family commitments, lessons, important school commitments—everything. Ask your child daily about any long-range dates that can be put on the calendar. You should also enter any family commitments that affect your child's schedule. It is especially important to enter vacation times, visits to grandparents, and so on. Schedules include fun events as well as work tasks.

Make positive comments each time a notation is made. Talk about how much easier it is to remember things when they are on the calendar. As your child gets older, encourage and guide him in writing his own notations on the calendar.

As it becomes appropriate, transfer the necessary items from the *Monthly Calendar* to the *Weekly Schedule* discussed in the next section.

Activities for Younger Children

For young children, filling in months and dates becomes its own learning experience. The activities that follow will provide opportunities to practice sequencing numbers, as well as spelling of the months and days. They will also demonstrate that not all months have the

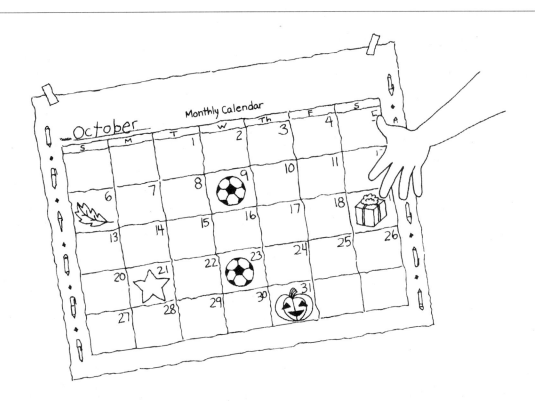

same number of days, nor do the dates always fall on the same days. These kinds of sequencing activities are valuable for later educational demands. Here are some specific activities that may help to introduce younger children to the idea of using a *Monthly Calendar*.

- ◆ Since younger children may not have the writing ability to describe their activities, have them make simple drawings instead. Discuss the activities for the month as they arise.

- ◆ Purchase a selection of colorful stickers with your child to represent activities on the *Monthly Calendar*. Encourage your child to place stickers in the proper places on the calendar as activities arise.

- ◆ For repetitive activities, purchase blank self-adhesive labels and have your child create a sketch to represent the activity on these labels. For example, you could make ten baseball labels to schedule Little League practices, or ten dancer labels to schedule ballet classes. Then just peel the labels and place them on the correct dates on the calendar.

As the child's scheduling demands increase, consider reducing the size of the *Monthly Calendar* on any copying machine. Give him a copy to keep with him as a handy reference to avoid conflicts. Suggest that you will keep a copy to remind you of your commitments to him. (This communicates that using a calendar is a grown-up thing to do!)

You also might consider sending a copy of your child's schedule—perhaps with a birthday card, a Christmas card, etc.—to grandparents or close friends. This will enhance the child's self-esteem and further family communications by showing all the activities in which he is involved.

The Organization Tools

The Weekly Schedule

Using the *Weekly Schedule* not only teaches children how to plan their time, it also helps them to learn how to establish priorities—what is most important to be done and what could wait. Transfer events from the *Daily Assignment Planner* and the *Monthly Calendar* to the *Weekly Schedule*. You will find a blank *Weekly Schedule* form to copy in the *Appendix*. This may be kept in a three-ring binder with the *Daily Assignment Planner*.

With your child's help each week, enter times of appointments, lessons, games, meetings, parties, friends' planned visits, chores, and other obligations. Remember to leave time for play and time for just relaxing and doing "nothing special." The *Weekly Schedule* is not intended to program every waking hour, but it is important for your child to begin to see how demands on his time must be organized.

Complete the *Weekly Schedule* in pencil, revising and updating as new activities arise and as events need to be rescheduled. Writing in pencil will allow for the frequent revision that will (and should) be needed.

Use the *Daily Assignment Planner* as the key source for the *Weekly Schedule*. If there is a spelling test on Friday, help your child to schedule the necessary studying time on Monday through Thursday. If a dental appointment and gymnastics meet are scheduled for Thursday, then Thursday is probably not the most efficient time to study for the spelling test. Looking at the week as a whole will help your child to understand that preparation time for that spelling test needs to be scheduled.

Help your child to enter specific study tasks in the *Weekly Schedule*, instead of just writing "study time." Research shows that studying is most efficient if done using short, specific study activities every night followed by a short review the night prior to the test. Be as specific as possible on the schedule. This encourages your child to plan what he must do during his studying. This develops good learning habits and will allow the child to know when he has finished. Specific planning will also enable your child to avoid "staring," which is an unproductive use of time and gives studying a bad image. Remember, *vaguely stated tasks*—"study," "do arithmetic," "do vocabulary"—*all encourage wasted time.*

Here are some examples of *specific* tasks:

> Write out 10 sentences for 10 spelling words.
>
> Practice drawing the life cycle of a frog.
>
> Do examples 1-10, p. 135, arithmetic.
>
> Write a paragraph using 10 vocabulary words.
>
> Practice the 7's table with a tape recorder.
>
> Listen to evening news and write a summary of 2 news items of national interest.

Here's another example. The word *spelling*, listed for 5:00-5:30 on Monday through Thursday, is not as efficient or productive as the following:

> Mon 5:00 spelling/10 words into tape recorder
>
> Tue 5:00 spelling/self-test and correct problem words/4 column sheet
>
> Wed 5:00 spelling/self-test problem words, self-test all words on tape
>
> Thu 5:00 spelling/review problem words/4 column sheet, self-test until 100%

A *Weekly Schedule* with specific tasks actually may mean less time spent studying, because much so-called "study time" is really unfocused staring.

Activities for Younger Children

The activities suggested for the *Monthly Calendar* will also work for the *Weekly Schedule*.

The Reading Tools

Chapter 2

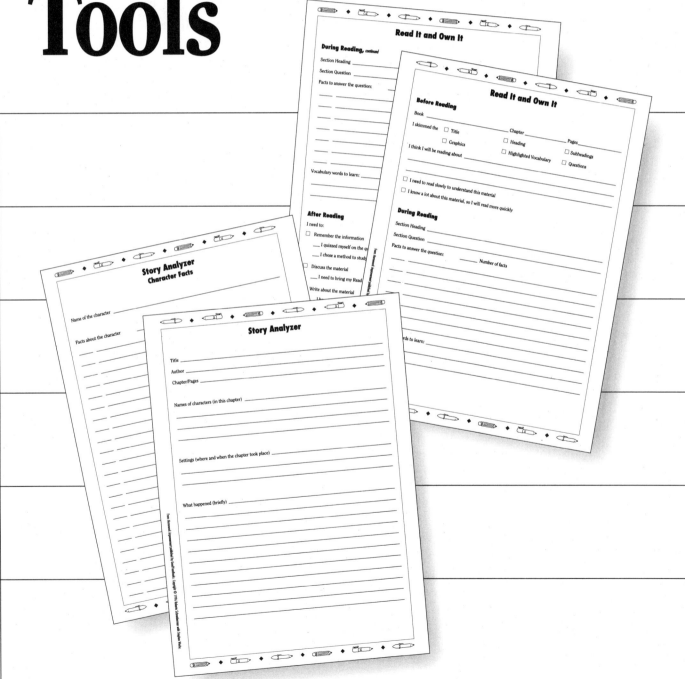

The Reading Tools

When educators say that children must learn to read, they mean that children must learn to understand what they read. The Reading Tool will maximize learning potential by helping your child to interpret what she reads.

The importance of reading is demonstrated every day in our lives—whether it's reacting to daily mail, following a recipe, or understanding directions for a new stereo. In all of these situations, we must go beyond merely seeing the words written on a piece of paper. We have to interpret those words and translate them into an action—paying a bill, producing a great dish, installing a new stereo.

It's the same with your child's reading. The ability to understand and interpret what is being read will maximize the potential for learning. She must not only understand the overall concept presented by the written words, she must also be able to identify any important information related to that concept. The tools and suggestions in this chapter will help you to help your child develop this habit.

Read It and Own It

Research over twenty years by the National Assessment of Educational Progress shows that most students can read at a surface level and comprehend the general meaning of the material. Many don't read analytically, however; many don't do well on reading assignments that are challenging. They can understand parts of what they read, but they have trouble fully understanding the main topic. They also have difficulty providing evidence from the reading material to support whatever understanding they have.

Despite our technological age, your child must still be able to understand and interpret what she reads if she is to maximize her learning potential. She must learn not only to see the overall idea being presented, but also to see, understand, and (often) remember the elements of that idea. In addition, she must learn to plan her reading, check her comprehension, and evaluate what she has learned.

Read It and Own It will enable your child to analyze content material such as that found in science and social studies readings.

Let's examine a typical content reading assignment and a typical student response. The student receives an assignment to read pages 23-25 in the world history book and be ready to talk about life in the Roman Empire.

What happens next is very common. Typically, the student sits at a table or lies on her bed and turns to the correct page. She begins to read the words, and the telephone rings. The call is for her; she speaks for a few minutes; Mom scolds and tells her to go back to her homework. She eventually hangs up and continues to read. During the reading process, she reads about temples, theaters, and public baths. Her mind starts to wander, perhaps back to the phone call. After a few moments, she refocuses and continues reading. Another ten or fifteen minutes passes, and she realizes that she has finished reading. She leaves her room. When questioned if she finished her homework, she shouts that she only had to read three pages for tomorrow.

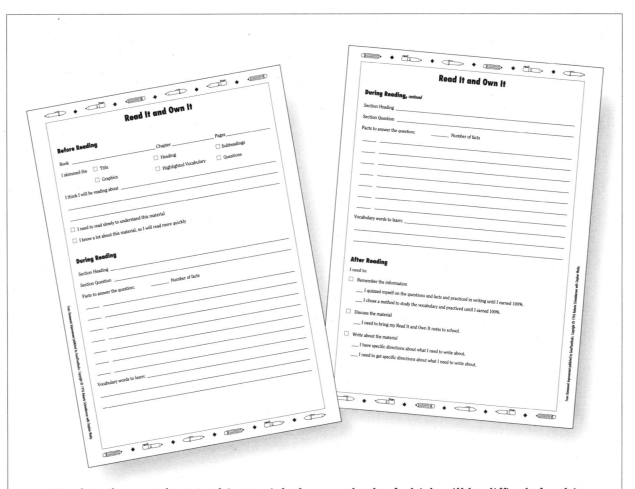

In class the next day two things might happen, both of which will be difficult for this child. First, she will hear the scariest eleven words in a student's life: "There will be a short surprise quiz on last night's reading." During the quiz, she remembers some of the ideas, but can't really answer very much. The question areas sound familiar, but she can't give specific answers. In the second, somewhat less discomforting, but just as revealing scenario, the teacher leads a discussion in class about last night's reading, and she is unable to answer any specific questions. The teacher even asks if she really read the material; she begins to wonder why she even bothers because it doesn't seem to make any difference. She never seems to have answers for the teacher's questions.

The *Read It and Own It* tool would have enabled this child to succeed at both of these tasks. How would she have performed? Let's look at this revised scenario.

Using the *Read It and Own It* tool, the child would have become actively involved in the reading process. She would have been asking herself questions, answering those questions both orally and in writing while she studied the material. She would have been studying with more than her eyes; as a result, at the end of the reading assignment, she would not find herself wondering what she had just read.

Here's why it works: As your child develops the ability to read words, *Read It and Own It* develops her ability to interpret what she reads. This tool forces the reader to plan her reading, check her understanding, and study what she has learned. It provides the student with a structure to improve her comprehension. When this tool is used correctly, your child, her teachers, and you will be astounded at how well she understands and remembers what she has read.

Here's how to use *Read It and Own It* with any factual material (social studies, science, etc.) at any grade level. (Blank forms are provided in the *Appendix* to copy.) Your child should proceed as follows:

Before Reading

Step 1: Fill in the identifying information for the reading assignment: book, chapter, and pages.

Step 2: Read the title, headings, subheadings, questions, graphics (pictures, charts, and graphs) and highlighted vocabulary (in bold print or italics) and check the appropriate boxes on the form verifying that this was completed.

Step 3: Think about what you read during Step 2 and predict what the reading assignment is about, writing your prediction on the lines provided.

Step 4: Decide if you have much knowledge about this material or if the material contains mostly new information. This is important to help you decide on your reading speed. Check the correct box for your reading speed.

This completes the *Before Reading* section of *Read It and Own It*. This section should not be ignored or skipped. It sets the purpose and speed of reading, and it activates your child's prior knowledge of the material. This allows her to interact appropriately with the text, which eliminates daydreaming.

During Reading

Step 5: Fill in the section heading (All content area textbooks have sections identified by headings in bold print).

Step 6: Convert the section heading into a question and enter that question on the section question line. (This establishes the purpose for reading this section; after reading the section, you should be able to answer the question. It may also be a question on a test!)

Step 7: Read the section. Every time you find a fact that will answer the question, you should write it in the "facts to answer the question" spaces on the form. (Important: Check a box for new fact, and skip a line between facts. If room runs out, continue in the next part of the form, ignoring the section identifications.)

Step 8: Pay special attention to new vocabulary words and list them in the vocabulary section for later study.

Step 9: When you finish the section, you should count the number of facts found and enter that number in the space under the section question.

Step 10: Continue this process for each of the sections in the reading assignment.

This completes the *During Reading* section. It allows your child to confirm, refine, or reject her predictions about the material. In addition, it provides a structure within which to search for information to answer questions, to distinguish important from unimportant information, to take written notes, and to highlight new vocabulary.

After Reading

After Reading activities depend on the purpose for reading.

- ◆ If the purpose is to remember the information, your child should: Cover the form with a blank sheet of paper so that only the information preceding the list of facts is visible. She should read the question and try to write the answer on the blank sheet of paper. The number of facts in the answer should match the number of facts entered on the form. Your child now realizes what she knows and what she doesn't and therefore what needs more study. In addition, she should study the vocabulary following the procedures listed under the *Practice Tool,* in Chapter 3.

- ◆ If the purpose for reading is to be ready to discuss the material, your child should: Take her *Read It and Own It* notes to school to use during class discussion. If your child has read the material carefully, she has interacted with it and formed opinions. Her opinions are valid only if she can back them up with facts. Because this is a problem area for many students, it causes them to wonder why they even bother reading, since they still can't fully participate in class discussions. The *Read It and Own It* notes will provide support for this important classroom activity.

- ◆ If the purpose for reading is to be ready to write about the material: Ask your child if the teacher was specific about what information was to be covered in the writing assignment. For example, she might be asked to compare and contrast two different aspects of the reading. If she cannot frame a written discussion along these lines, her writing may not conform to the teacher's expectations, and she will once again become discouraged and start to wonder why she bothered to read the selection.

The Reading Tools

Read It and Own It

Before Reading

Book _Ancient Civilizations_ Chapter _3_ Pages _23-25_

I skimmed the:
- ☑ Title
- ☑ Heading
- ☑ Subheadings
- ☑ Highlighted Vocabulary
- ☑ Questions
- ☑ Graphics

I think I will be reading about _Ancient cities and what they were like._

- ☑ I need to read slowly to understand this material
- ☐ I know a lot about this material, so I will read more quickly

During Reading

Section Heading _Importance of the cities_
Section Question _Why were the cities important?_
Facts to answer the question: _3_ Number of facts

- ✓ _they protected people's freedom_
- ✓ _because of freedom, new cities sprang up and old ones took on a new life_
- ✓ _political, social, and cultural life were in the cities_

Vocabulary words to learn: _cardo   decumanus   periphery_

Read It and Own It

During Reading, _continued_

Section Heading _Luxury of City Life_
Section Question _What was luxurious about city life?_
Facts to answer the question: _3_ Number of facts

- ✓ _splendid temples, theaters, circuses, forums, public baths, and palaces_
- ✓ _streets wide and clean_
- ✓ _aqueducts brought water to the city_

Vocabulary words to learn: _basilicas   mercantile   utilitarian_

After Reading

I need to:
- ☑ Remember the information
  - ✓ I quizzed myself on the questions and facts and practiced in writing until I earned 100%.
  - ✓ I chose a method to study the vocabulary and practiced until I earned 100%.
- ☑ Discuss the material
  - ✓ I need to bring my Read It and Own It notes to school.
- ☐ Write about the material
  - — I have specific directions about what I need to write about.
  - — I need to get specific directions about what I need to write about.

If you are unable to help her specify the writing assignment through questioning or by having her call another student, you should discuss this issue with her teacher. Hidden assignments almost always end in failure.

Once the writing assignment is clear, have your child produce a written composition based on the material she read. The *Read It and Own It* form will contain facts needed in the composition.

This completes the *After Reading* section. It provides a structure in which your child can think about the next requirement associated with the reading and determine the appropriate strategy to meet that requirement. Dependent upon the *After Reading* strategy chosen, she will increase her retention, gain additional control over her writing, increase her confidence level, and be able to defend her opinions during class discussion.

Here are the benefits of the *Read It and Own It* system:

◆ provides structure to improve comprehension of content area textbooks

◆ establishes a format for active involvement in the reading process

◆ highlights the three parts of content reading: pre-reading, during reading, and after reading activities

◆ eliminates parent questioning—your child will know if she is ready for the discussion, the test, or the writing assignment

Read It and Own It will increase your child's confidence as her grades and her class participation soar. Your child will be in charge of her own learning. She will be ready to work with the additional instruction in school to expand her knowledge into the areas of making inferences and generalizations. In addition, she will be open to instruction about expanded methods of reading instruction for varying types of material, based on her particular learning style.

Story Analyzer

The *Story Analyzer* includes two forms to help your child study stories. The *Story Analyzer* can be used for all kinds of fiction—short stories or novels—as well as for nonfiction that has the elements of characters and setting, such as biographies.

The *Story Analyzer* forces the reader to focus on three elements of literature while reading: the characters (who is in the story), the settings (all the places and times in which the story takes place), and the plot (primary events). Through simultaneous reading and analysis, your child will develop a packet of information about the literature to enable her to review and study without rereading and to be prepared for classroom discussions that analyze the literature. Reproducible *Story Analyzer* forms are located in the *Appendix*.

Here is how to use the Story Analyzer:

Step 1: Fill in the identifying information: title, author, chapter, or pages.

The Reading Tools

As the child is reading, have her follow the three literary elements in the following ways:

Characters:

List the characters in each chapter on the *Story Analyzer* form. Then complete a *Character Facts* form for every character listed. Each time your child discovers something about the character, have her list it on that character's fact sheet. Remind your child to list only words and phrases and not complete sentences. These should not be detailed character descriptions, just one- or two-word descriptions of the character—such as mean, quiet, smart, and so forth.

Keep in mind that some characters will become unimportant as the story progresses, but the reader won't know the importance or unimportance of the character at the time he or she first appears. Your child should list all of the characters as they are introduced and determine their importance later. (One clue to a character's unimportance will be a scarcity of information about the character on the *Character Facts* form.)

Settings:

Every time the setting (time or place) changes, your child should list the new setting in the *Settings* section of the form. Like the characters, some of the changes in settings will turn out to be unimportant, but this will not be known until after the setting actually changes and the reader discovers what has occurred. So it is important to write down all of the changes in settings and determine their importance later.

What Happened:

Every time any of the characters becomes involved in a new situation, have your child list that situation in as few words as possible in the *What Happened* section of the form. These should not be detailed descriptions of the occurrences, just one or two words that will *remind* the child of the situations—words such as *the storm, the party, the big fight,* and so forth. You might even suggest a sketch to represent these happenings. Remember that you just want to create a reference point to trigger memory; the form doesn't matter.

Use a new *Story Analyzer* form for each chapter.

Step 2: When she has finished reading the short story or book, your child should count the number of facts found for each character and enter that number in the box provided on the *Character Facts* form.

Your child may take her *Story Analyzer* notes to school for reference during class discussions or for specific information when reacting to the material in writing. This enables her to have a source of information, with a reference to location within the book, when discussions or writing assignments occur. Students often read for pleasure and are unable to remember or locate specifics for later story discussion in class. They then feel discouraged when they decide that their only solution is to reread the entire story or book.

The *Story Analyzer* provides a system to keep notations during reading, which can be easily accessed as class demands are presented. If your child will be tested on the material, she will have ready a complete and organized review document. She will have specific material to use when studying in addition to the material provided by the teacher on such concepts as theme and point of view.

Here is how the material should be used to study for the test:

Step 1: Reread the *Story Analyzer* packet to establish a feeling for it as a whole. It is most helpful to do this aloud. Reading aloud increases concentration and for many children this is often the most helpful way to remember material.

You will have to guide your child through this process. Later, she will be comfortable and competent doing this alone. You, as a parent, will have established the method, and strong test grades will have established the reward.

Step 2: Read each subsection *(Characters, Settings, What Happened)* and elaborate orally, in as much detail as possible, on what is written. Any time a notation does not trigger memory, go back to the specific chapter for clarification.

Step 3: Cover all the facts about a character on the *Character Facts* sheet with a blank piece of paper. Your child should read the name and try to write as many facts about that character as possible on the blank piece of paper. (Remember to use a thick or doubled piece of paper, so that memory is truly being tested!) The number of facts in the answer should match as closely as possible the number of facts entered in the box on the form. This process will help your child identify which characters she knows and which need additional study time.

Many students become familiar with the characters in a story, but find that under the pressure of testing and or writing they forget or confuse one character with aspects of another character. Working with the *Character Facts* sheet helps eliminate this problem.

Additional Applications

Many times students are expected to read a series of short stories around a central theme. Following the conclusion of the unit, they are tested on the theme as illustrated in the individual stories.

Many students find these units confusing. They will claim that they can't attribute characters and plots to the correct stories. The *Story Analyzer* prevents this from happening by allowing the student to review a literature unit with the same confidence as for individual books by completing one analyzer for each story.

Activities for Younger Children

Although it is widely recognized that the home environment has a strong impact on a child's academic achievement, research shows that too many students report receiving little support at home for reading. You, as a parent, can change this for your child. Encourage leisure reading by:

- reading in front of your children to set a model
- limiting family television viewing time and substituting family reading time in its place
- visiting the library and bookstore
- reading to your children even if they are capable of reading by themselves
- discussing what they are reading and asking for their personal reactions to their reading
- helping them to gather more information about interesting topics

In a home that loves books, children get the message that education is important and supported at home. You are their first and most important role model. Children learn vocabulary by reading, they learn about a multitude of ideas by reading, and they can stretch their imagination by visualizing what they read. You can support the efforts of the school and contribute in great part to your child's success by promoting reading activities in your home.

Technology has found its way into many homes in the form of computers. Word processors offer a wonderful way for parents to help their children expand their thinking skills.

The Reading Tools

Suggest to your child that she retell a story—a movie seen recently, a book read aloud, a TV sitcom that was particularly enjoyed—to someone who didn't see it. Follow the steps in the *Story Analyzer* by asking your child questions designed to elicit descriptions of characters, setting, and plot.

> Who was in the story? (Characters)
>
> Where did the story happen? What kind of day was it? (Setting)
>
> What happened? Then what happened? (Plot)

As this process unfolds, your child will learn how to organize thoughts around a structure that she will need to understand more advanced reading.

Here is another suggestion:

When your child says she has nothing to do, or at a time when she is between activities, tell her to make up a story. Young children often do this. When your child tells you a story about her favorite TV character, ask her to tell a new story using the same character. Or, change the ending of the story, put the character in a different place, give the character a new problem to solve, make yourself one of the characters. Use the same techniques to help your child to incorporate characters, setting, and plot. Ask her to illustrate her story and share it with a younger child. You could be encouraging the next great novelist!

The Practice Tools

Chapter 3

The Practice Tools

The old saw "Practice makes perfect" is true. If your child had nothing to do all day but study spelling words, his spelling tests would be perfect. But what about the rest of his life?

The *Practice Tools* in *Homework Improvement* not only provide methods for practice, they make studying fast and efficient. Maximum learning can be accomplished in minimum time.

Perhaps the most important aspect of the *Practice Tools* is that they provide flexibility for studying. There are too many children for whom studying—practice—consists of only a single method. If it fails, they fail and claim that studying doesn't help. As learning demands increase with age, your child needs to be more flexible in the practice methods he chooses. He needs to know that there is more than one way to study and when each method is appropriate.

As you begin using the *Practice Tools*, you should help your child to select the most efficient tool—the one that matches the way he will be tested on that material. Very soon, he will be making that decision without your help. You will have given him the ability to determine which study method is most appropriate.

The multimethod approach means fewer surprises at test time. Your child has studied what the teacher will be evaluating and—most importantly—in the same format. Under these circumstances, grades soar.

Flash Cards

Flash Cards are among the most commonly used methods of self-study. *Flash Cards* help drill the association between two related pieces of information: a vocabulary word and its definition, an abbreviation and its meaning, a date with a fact, a diagram and its labels, and so on. Since many student tests revolve around providing a specific piece of information given a prompt, *Flash Cards* can be useful in many situations. *Flash Cards* can be made of any paper large enough to accommodate all the written information needed on both sides, but small enough to be held in a child's hand.

Flash Cards are an exceptionally useful tool, but many students use them incorrectly. Students often discover *Flash Cards* early in their learning years and try to use them for everything. Incorrect use, however, frequently produces less than satisfactory results, despite the value of this tool.

The most frequent misuse of *Flash Cards* occurs when children do not make a concerted effort to separate the facts they know from those they don't know. Flipping quickly through the cards, the child sees many facts he knows and spends the most time with those, because they are familiar. He is quick to check the backs of the cards for information that did not come readily, but does not separate those cards out and spend additional time with them. In this way, students delude themselves into thinking they know the material. The session finally ends with boredom when the student convinces himself that he knows everything.

At test time, this poor study method leads to frustration. The teacher may list ten words for the student to define and ten definitions for which he must write the correct words. He

can't remember the exact definition for some words. When given the definitions, he might even become angry when asked to write the words, because he didn't study them that way.

These rules for the successful use of *Flash Cards* allow your child to evaluate his knowledge, to determine what he knows and what he doesn't know, and to judge how much more time should be spent to become fully competent.

- ◆ Don't use *Flash Cards* as the first method of learning associations. Use them only for associations that are problems during study. (See *Split Sheets* in this chapter.) This strategy becomes more useful when older students need to learn 50, 60, or 100 different associations for a test. Monitor the use of flash cards.

- ◆ Drill in both directions. This simple technique will virtually guarantee total mastery.

- ◆ Talk aloud as the cards are turned over (even when studying alone). This allows your child to check responses better and reinforces the visual aspect of the drill using multi-sensory learning.

- ◆ Separate known associations from unknown associations. Don't waste study time on associations already known. Devote time to the associations that really need study. (See *Sorting Boxes* in this chapter.)

- ◆ Ask your child to write out answers, even for associations he knows verbally. This reinforces the information and may be the form in which your child is asked to demonstrate knowledge. (Most tests are written.) If your child is unable to write out the correct answer, then the card should go into a sorting box for unknown matches.

(You will find a description of the *Sorting Box* later in this chapter. See *Four-Column Sheets* for a way to study associations that prove especially difficult.)

◆ Repeat the flash card process until your child can write all of the associations correctly in both directions.

Be creative. Encourage your child to think of ways to use this method to foster active learning.

When you teach your child how to use *Flash Cards*, he is studying independently—evaluating what he knows, receiving immediate feedback, identifying the problem areas, checking the spelling—and all in the form in which he will be evaluated!

The *Appendix* includes a sheet of blank *Flash Cards* that you can easily reproduce. After copying, simply separate by cutting on the bold black lines and create *Flash Cards* as needed.

Matching Deck

Another associative learning tool, *Matching Deck* differs from *Flash Cards* in that it provides practice in selecting the right answer from a list of possibilities.

Remember that the study method needs to match the testing method as closely as possible. That way, the test will seem just like the study sessions. That's why it is important for you to question your child about the testing format, until such time as he understands that the testing and study formats need to match.

It is important that your child understand that the study method needs to match the test method. Prior to helping him determine which study method is best, you need to determine the testing method. It may be that neither flash cards nor matching decks is appropriate if, for example, he needs to write the word in the test. In that case, he should be using the *Four-Column Sheet* or a *Split Sheet,* described later in this chapter. Choose the tool carefully for best results.

Using the *Matching Deck* form included in the *Appendix*, have your child list the two items to be associated on the same side of attached cards instead of on the front and back of the same card as in *Flash Cards*. Number the reverse side on both halves, so that when the two halves are separated they can be associated both by the information on one side and by the identical numbers on the other.

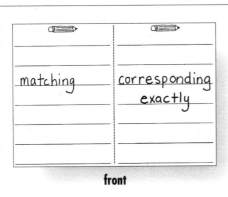
front

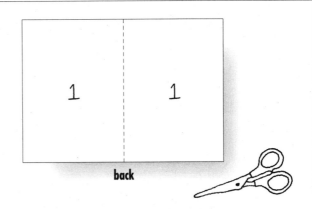
back

Once your child has put the two pieces of matching information on the fronts and the same numbers on the backs, cut the cards on the dotted lines to create two separate cards that together form a match.

The key to using the *Matching Deck* is to introduce the pairs of matching information to the child's learning process gradually, instead of presenting them all at once.

Here's how to use the *Matching Deck* after it's been constructed.

Step 1: Select any pair at random from the prepared cards and have your child read both items aloud.

Step 2: Discuss how to remember the association (see *Word Associations* in Chapter 6).

Step 3: Select another pair at random and discuss how to remember this second association.

Step 4: Place all the cards on a table with the numbers facing down (not visible).

Step 5: Mix the cards.

Step 6: Have your child pick any card at random and find its match.

Step 7: Confirm each match by checking the numbers on the backs.

Step 8: If correct, remove those cards and set them aside.

Continue Steps 3 through 8 until all cards you have created have been incorporated into the *Matching Deck*.

Stop each round before the child begins to guess at the associations. Remember that the choices become narrower as correct matches are made and eliminated from the cards on the table. If correct matching continues to the end, the last two cards on the table must be a match and will be correct whether the child knows the association or not. That's why you need to repeat the "final challenge" (all the cards on the table) more than once to ensure that your child knows and remembers each association.

Matching Decks encourage concentration and increase attention spans. While involved in matching, your child is physically searching for the correct match—overturning cards in the process. Young minds become more focused and are less likely to wander when physical activity accompanies mental activity.

The Practice Tools

Encourage your child to use *Matching Decks* for all kinds of associations. They Have a game-like character that kids love.

Sorting Boxes

Sorting Boxes, which are used with *Flash Cards* and *Matching Decks*, focus the child on efficient learning. *Sorting Boxes* are simple to use and understand, but they teach an enormously important concept. That concept is:

> Concentrate your study time on the information that needs studying—information that's unknown. Don't waste time studying what you already know.

Sorting Boxes teach children how to separate material they need to learn from information they already know. Additional boxes can be made to sort finished/unfinished, important/unimportant, need/want, and so forth. Later in life, other devices will replace sorting boxes—piles of pages, folders, envelopes, or other ways of physically separating material. Your child will have learned this useful organizational concept early on.

It is important to praise your child for using the *Unknown* box. Tell your child that it's good to recognize what he doesn't know, so that the information can be learned. Once the

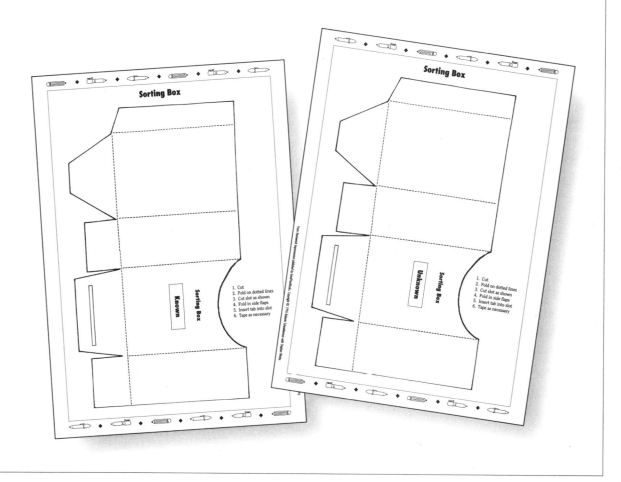

concept of categorization is understood (some children understand it after the first couple of tests), it will become natural behavior. He will have learned a valuable lesson for school and for life.

Sorting Box templates are found in the *Appendix*. They should be cut from sturdy cardboard for stability. Simply cut, fold, and insert tabs. Your child is now ready to proceed efficiently with *Flash Cards* and/or *Matching Decks* by placing the cards into the correct box while studying.

Activities for Younger Children

Contrasting helps us to separate two items or ideas. You can start your children early in understanding separation by contrasting physical qualities—dark colors from light, hard things from soft, etc. Once that is understood you can separate ideas—fun things to do from not-such-fun things to do, weather that's nice and weather that's not, etc. This activity is excellent preparation for future outlining and categorizing—important skills for all aspects of later learning. It is to a young child what file folders are to adults!

Split Sheets

As early as third grade, students often receive assignments to define vocabulary words. The assignments, if completed correctly, become wonderful tools for studying. If done incorrectly, they fulfill no other purpose than homework completion. *Split Sheets* encourage the most efficient completion of this type of assignment. Using *Split Sheets* saves study time, because the homework assignment becomes the study tool. In other words, a homework

The Practice Tools

> serape — a colorful woolen shawl worn over the shoulders by Mexican men
>
> sombrero — a wide-brimmed hat
>
> siesta — a nap usually taken in mid-afternoon
>
> tortillas — corn cakes
>
> petate — straw sleeping mat
>
> rebozo — shawl for carrying things on the back, such as babies
>
> tierra caliente — "hot land," the land near sea level and the lower edges of the mountains where it is always warm

Figure 1 A typical MEXICO unit vocabulary assignment as completed by many students, regardless of grade level or ability level

assignment—writing out definitions of vocabulary words, for example—can also be used to study for the test on that material.

The special format used by *Split Sheets* relies on the separation of the words from the definitions. *Split Sheets* work because the easiest way for a child to study words and definitions is to arrange them in separate columns on a single piece of paper. That way, one column can be covered while the other is studied, and learning can be done in both directions. Note how much easier it is to study the *Split Sheet* in Figure 2 than the list in Figure 1.

Try to imagine what your child would do with a vocabulary assignment similar to this one. Most children just grab a piece of paper and write out the definitions as illustrated in Figure 1. Then they stare at the words and magically announce, "I'm through studying. I know the words." In reality however, such unfocused studying doesn't help at test time.

Try this with your child. Have him look at Figure 2 and study it for a few minutes. Now have him cover the second column (the definitions) with a piece of paper. On a blank piece of

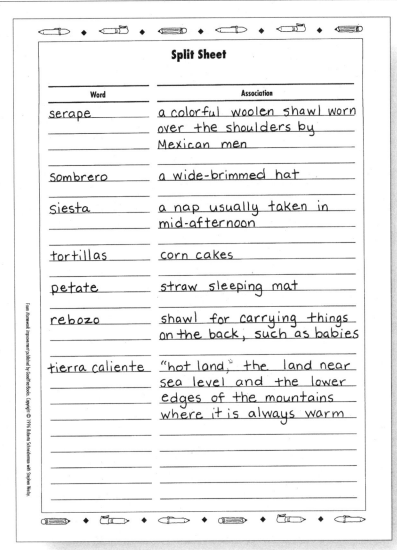

Figure 2 A typical MEXICO unit vocabulary assignment as completed using a Split Sheet

paper have him write each definition from memory. Now cover the words and, on a blank piece of paper, have him write the words with their correct spellings. It will be clear which words and definitions your child knows and which need further study.

Without *Split Sheets*, both words and definitions are visible during study, a situation that gives hints, resulting in an inflated evaluation of what the student really knows. This false assessment will mean that information is not retained, and this will likely lead to a low grade at test time when the clues are no longer available.

Using *Split Sheets*, your child can easily test himself and determine which words to study more intensely using the other tools in this book: *Flash Cards, Matching Deck, Four-Column Pages,* or *Word Associations.*

Here's how to use *Split Sheets*, found in the *Appendix* and ready for you to copy. Have your child record the assigned words and definitions on the *Split Sheets*, skipping lines between entries to separate ideas. If the teacher usually collects this homework and does not return it for studying, your child can use carbon paper or you can photocopy the assignment. If the teacher only checks to see that it was completed, you don't need a copy.

At study time, your child is ready for self-study, following these steps:

Step 1: Cover the first column of words with a blank piece of paper (thick enough to prevent hints from showing through)

Step 2: Write the hidden words opposite each exposed definition.

Step 3: Continue through the entire list.

Step 4: Remove the piece of paper and compare written answers to the original.

Step 5: Mark exact answers correct and mark incomplete, vague, or wrong answers as errors.

Step 6: Reverse the process, using another folded sheet of paper to now cover the definitions.

Step 7: Use *Flash Cards*, *Matching Deck*, or *Four-Column Sheets* to learn the unknowns.

Using *Split Sheets*, your child both completes his homework and produces an efficient study tool. The applications are endless, and the technique is practical at all levels of learning. *Split Sheets* will help your child to evaluate his learning and know when he has mastered the information. Your child will decide when and for what assignments it should be used. Best of all, it's done independently.

Four-Column Pages

The *Four-Column Page* is an effective tool to help your child conquer associations independently. Associations can be anything from vocabulary words to arithmetic problems, spelling words to history facts, and even beyond. The *Four-Column Page* is based on the philosophy that if you want to remember something, you write it repeatedly. With *Four-Column Pages*, your child must finish the repetition of each unknown association before starting the next one. Remember that this should not be used for every problem association, just the ones that can't be conquered in other ways. It's too time-consuming to be used every time.

Here's how it works:

Step 1: Place the two items to be associated (spelling and meaning, word and definition, word and association) in the first two columns of the *Four-Column Page*. That leaves two blank columns on the sheet.

Step 2: Fold back the first column (the one with the word *clothing* in our example) to leave only the second column visible (the one with the word *apparel*).

Step 3: Guide your child to use the information that he can see in the second column (the word *apparel*) to remember the hidden half of the association and then to write it in the next empty column.

Step 4: Instruct your child to unfold the *Four-Column Page* at this point to check the accuracy of his answers against the first column.

If the answer is correct, continue. If the answer is incorrect, help your child to correct it. Initially you may have to assist, but after a few minutes he should continue on his own.

Step 5: Once the correct answer has been established, fold the first two columns back. Only two columns should be visible.

Have your child enter the corresponding association in the last empty column.

Step 6: Unfold to reveal the first two columns and check for accuracy.

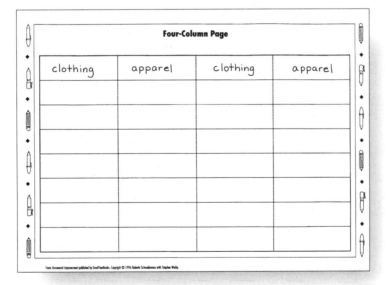

Turn the page over and repeat the entire process. Remember that your child can never do this incorrectly as long as only one filled-in column is visible at a time. Other visible columns should be blank.

As a result of this drill, your child will have memorized this association and should now be able to return to his original practice tool (*Flash Cards, Matching Deck, Split Sheets*) for a perfect score!

Parents of young children also will find this method helpful. Even your six- or seven-year-old will be able to study without your help, after you've shown him how.

Activities for Younger Children

Associative learning strategies are among the most important learning techniques you can teach to your children. You should start early by using *Flash Cards* or *Matching Decks* to teach them basic ideas that they will need for life—telling time, remembering a birthday, money concepts, measurements. Of course, there are school uses too, even at a young age. Here are some ideas for younger children for which you can use either *Flash Cards* or a *Matching Deck*. (Important: Follow all the rules above, even when working with younger children).

Reading sight words:

Put a word on one side of the card and a hand-drawn or magazine picture on the other side. You can help make the first *Flash Cards* or *Matching Decks*, but even first-graders can make their own cards and most eight- or nine-year-olds should be encouraged to drill alone.

- **State and country names and shapes:** Trace the shape of the state or country from an atlas on one side and write the name on the other.

- **States and countries and their capitals:** Write the state or country on one side and the capital on the other.

- **Contractions:** Write the contraction on one side (isn't, for example) and the full words (is not) on the other.

- **Uppercase and lowercase letters:** Many children have difficulty remembering the lowercase forms of letters, and they will use a capital letter in the middle of a word. If your child has this problem, use *Flash Cards* or a *Matching Deck* to reinforce the correct associations. Use these methods to establish associations between manuscript and cursive forms of letters.

- **Telling time:** Write the time in numbers on one side and a clock face of the time on the other side. An additional useful step would be to try to duplicate the clock face while looking at the time in numbers.

- **Linear measurements:** Put a picture of a portion of a ruler on one side of the card and the correct measurement on the other side of the card. (Hint: Use a photocopy of a ruler on one side of the card, marking the spot to be read.)

- **Recognition of coins and making change:** Photocopy coin combinations and tape them to the cards.

- ◆ **Phonetic sounds:** Place letter combinations on one side of the flash card and pictures of objects using the letter combination on the other. This will both confirm the correct sound and provide a memory trigger to assist your child in retrieving the sound.

- ◆ **Events and dates (personal or historical):** historical dates and their corresponding events are a natural for *Flash Cards* and *Matching Decks*. However, you can instill the idea of associative learning tools with younger children by using the tools to remember family events, birthdays, anniversaries, personal achievements, and so forth.

- ◆ **Sports:** If your child likes sports, he'll have fun using *Flash Cards* or *Matching Decks* to expand his knowledge of facts—players and teams, teams and cities, statistics, and so on.

Puzzle Charts

Using *Puzzle Charts*, you can help your child construct a game which will help him learn several interrelated facts or ideas about one general topic. Before information can be remembered, it must be understood. The best way to make sure information is understood is to place it into a chart in an organized fashion.

The ability to organize facts is a crucial skill required in notetaking and later learning. The best way to ensure that information is understood is to have your child make an organized chart of the information.

The list of uses for this tool is endless: the causes of a war; the characters, setting, theme, and plot of a story; examples of different forms of plant or animal life; and so on.

It's easy to see how to organize information for a *Puzzle Chart*. After you've done it, all you need is a pair of scissors. A blank chart is included in the *Appendix*.

Puzzle Charts have two sections: one sheet for writing and verifying and a carbon copy to be cut on the dotted lines. Your child will scatter and mix the pieces on the table and then re-create the original chart.

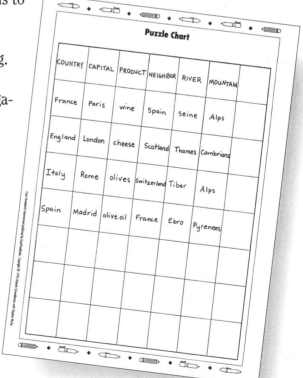

Here is an example of a Puzzle Chart created for a typical elementary level social studies class.

COUNTRY	CAPITAL	PRODUCT	NEIGHBOR	RIVER	MOUNTAIN
France	Paris	wine	Spain	Seine	Alps
England	London	cheese	Scotland	Thames	Cambrians
Italy	Rome	olives	Switzerland	Tiber	Alps
Spain	Madrid	olive oil	France	Ebro	Pyrenees

Here are the steps:

Step 1: Discuss with your child the relationships between the facts. (Every country has a capital, a river, a product, etc.) Once the concept is understood, begin constructing the chart.

Step 2: Place a piece of carbon paper between two *Puzzle Charts*. Create the chart on the top sheet.

Step 3: Detach top sheet. This is the answer sheet.

Step 4: Cut the *Puzzle Chart* copy along the dotted lines. Mix the pieces on the table.

Step 5: Re-create the original chart without looking at it.

Step 6: Check the reconstruction against the answer sheet.

Step 7: Repeat if necessary. Encourage your child to stay with it until he can duplicate the answer sheet.

Step 8: Re-create the chart from memory on a blank piece of paper.

When he can reconstruct the *Puzzle Charts*, your child's learning on this is complete. Since the child can reconstruct the chart from memory, using these facts in a test situation should be no problem. (See *Sneak-a-Peek Sheets* in Chapter 6.)

Once again (as with the *Matching Deck*) the combination of thinking and physical involvement enhances learning.

Activities for Younger Children

Puzzle Charts are like a game and kids love to use a game format for *studying;* just be prepared to stop when your child is ready to stop. Forcing the ideas won't help. Praise your child's drawing and imagination frequently. Display results on the refrigerator, on the wall, or by laminating copies and using them as place mats.

You can instill the idea of categorization in younger children by constructing the following *Puzzle Chart* and asking your child to find items that fit the cross-description—something that is round and red, or funny-shaped and blue, for example. In this puzzle chart, you can change any of the characteristics. Substitute locations, initial letters, physical properties, or other characteristics for colors

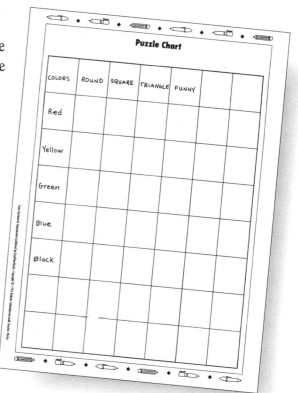

and shapes: tell the child to find something that is yellow and in the kitchen, find something that is square and starts with *R,* and so forth.

Stimulate your child's imagination by having him draw or find pictures of the object described by each of a pair of words—old toys, scary animals, and so on. While he is having fun thinking about these new objects, he will also be learning the idea of categorizing items by specific criteria. Tell him that there are no right answers here, he can make up the objects if he wants to; in fact, the more he uses his imagination, the more fun it will be!

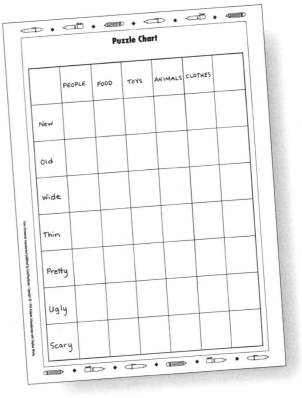

Chapter 4

The Writing Tools

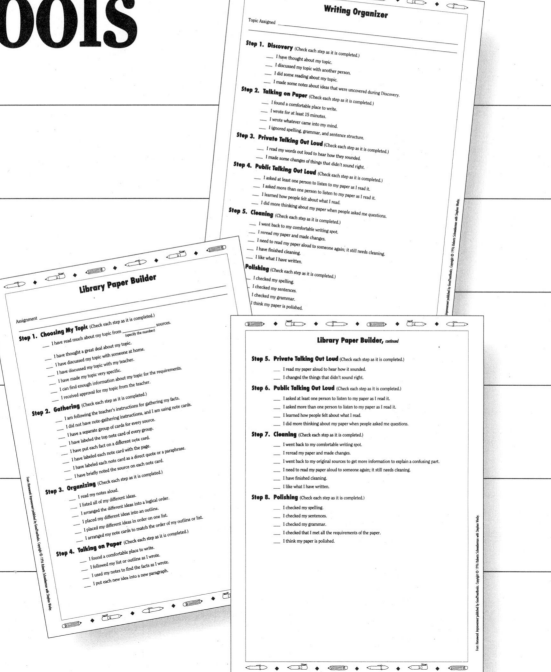

The Writing Tools

Complaints that today's children can't write well have nothing to do with handwriting. They concern children's inability to express thoughts—to communicate thoughts—in writing.

When teachers give writing assignments or essays, kids plunge right in. They don't think about what they want to say. They just begin writing, and any thought that enters their heads at a given moment ends up as the next sentence on the paper. Some students will write five disjointed sentences. Others will ramble on for five pages. Neither will meet expectations if they don't follow the correct process. So it's no wonder that writing assignments often are uninteresting and difficult to understand.

Many parents could write the assignment for their child if they wanted to do so. The vast majority of parents, however, don't know how to guide their child through the writing process.

The *Writing Tool* helps you to lead your child easily through anything from the simplest writing assignment to a research paper. After you've guided the process once or twice, your child will be able to do it alone. She will be able to produce more cohesive and organized writing assignments using the tools in this chapter.

The *Writing Organizer* and the *Library Paper Builder* lead your child through step-by-step processes that take only a few minutes of focused thinking before writing. Yet, with these tools she will craft more organized paragraphs, cohesive essays, and superior term papers.

Writing Organizer

The ability to communicate ideas in an organized fashion is a crucial skill that must be developed as early as possible and nurtured throughout the school years. When a child asks for help at home, many parents feel they are unable to assist satisfactorily. They may be able to suggest a topic. But how can they actually guide their child through the writing process without writing the assignment themselves?

The *Writing Organizer* will guide your child through her writing assignments and inspire more individualized and interesting paragraphs, essays, and papers. The *Appendix* contains a blank organizer form ready for copying.

Consider this example to help you understand the benefits of the *Writing Organizer*. Your fourth-grader receives the following assignment, due in three days: "Write about the funniest thing that ever happened to you." Your child has asked you for help.

Think about this writing assignment using the *Writing Organizer*.

Step 1: Discovery

Before your child can begin writing, she needs to think about her topic. You can help this thinking process by encouraging her to remember funny things that have happened to her. As she remembers the incidents, you may simply discuss them, or you may want to suggest that your child note them down on a piece of paper for further thinking. She may want to discuss the topic with friends or family members as a way to evoke memories.

Step 2: Talking on Paper

Getting those first words onto paper is often the hardest part! Your child wonders, How do I begin? What do I say? Suggest that your child not worry because her beginning and the way she says things will probably change as she writes. Tell her to find a quiet, comfortable place where she likes to think. Tell her to just "talk on paper" and write whatever comes into her mind about her topic.

Suggest that she should try to write for about fifteen minutes and not to worry about it making sense, if words are spelled correctly, or if she is writing in complete sentences. That will come later! Tell her to write anything that comes into her mind: a word, a phrase, things that people have said, or how she feels at the time. Explain that her job is to make you, her audience, understand this incident.

Step 3: Private Talking Out Loud

The first audience should be the author, your child. In this step the child needs to read aloud what she has written.

"Talking out loud" is important! Listening to her voice inside her head will not work as well. In this step she is no longer the writer. She becomes the audience, so she must really be able to hear the words.

Tell her to listen for words and phrases that don't sound right, or that are not really accurate, or for incomplete thoughts about the situation or the people or the events. This step should suggest some revisions that should be made at this point.

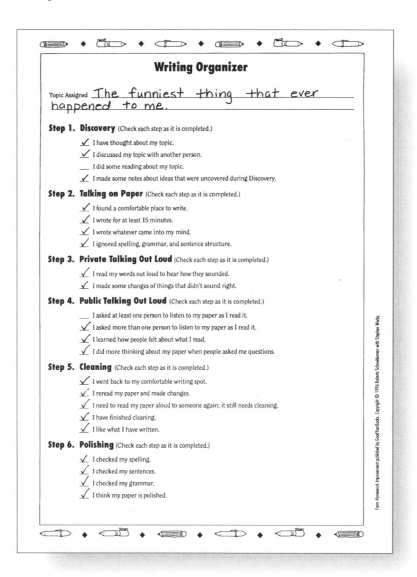

Step 4: Public Talking Out Loud

After your young author finishes "talking on paper" and "talking out loud," she should try "talking out loud" to someone else. You or other family members can now act as her next audience. Ask her to read it aloud to you. If she feels uncomfortable, tell her that the purpose is to make sure that other people can understand the story. If she still feels uncomfortable, you can read it aloud. Tell her how you feel about what she wrote. Ask her questions. This will allow her to think more about her writing and to think about the changes that will make her story clearer.

Step 5: Cleaning

Suggest that she now can go back to her comfortable writing spot and begin the "cleaning" process—the process of incorporating the revisions suggested by the "talking out loud" steps into her composition. Guide her to reread the paper, cross out as needed, reword, and explain further.

Some papers may need little work at this point; some papers may need major revisions. This is part of the process. Explain to your child that all writers go through the cleaning process. That is what makes people want to read what they have written.

Step 6: Polishing

During this last step, you and your child can look at spelling, grammar, and sentence structure. You can help your child decide what needs to be polished and allow her to do the polishing, or you can suggest that your child complete this task with her teacher when she has done as much as possible by herself. It's important that you don't do the correcting, thereby acting as the teacher. You're the guide, not the instructor throughout this process.

The *Writing Organizer* allows you to help your child through the writing process so that her own voice comes through in the writing. It provides a consistent and easy system to follow, regardless of the nature of the writing assignment. The process will grow with her as her writing demands increase and she will refine the steps to meet her working style, but you will have given her the foundation for knowing how to speak on paper. Her writing will now be interesting and individual.

A child who is comfortable with a short writing assignment will be equipped with the correct tools and attitudes for longer, more demanding papers.

Library Paper Builder

Your role as a facilitator is also important when your child is writing longer papers. Some schools call them library research papers, while others call them term papers. Too often, parents first learn late the night before that a paper is due the next day. The cry for help is there, but neither the time nor the plan exists to complete the project. The *Library Paper Builder* provides a plan so that such last-minute problems are less likely to occur. A blank form can be found in the *Appendix*.

Here's how the Library Paper Builder works.

Step 1: Choosing the Topic

This is difficult for students because they are usually given a wide range of choices. The way to narrow the choices is through reading and thinking. You can be most helpful at this point by providing encouragement. Encourage your child to read a little in each of the subject areas so that she can develop a general feeling for each topic.

Assure your child that it may take her some time to decide on her topic, and that this is acceptable. Encourage her to discuss her reading with other people, including her teacher and you, before she finally settles on a topic and the particular aspect of the topic that she wants to write about.

Once she has chosen a specific topic, ensure that she can locate enough information to meet the requirements of the library paper assignment. Make sure that the teacher approves of her specific topic. Too many students skip this very necessary step.

Step 2: Gathering

Your child should now begin in an organized fashion to gather the information from a variety of sources. Most teachers will specify the way in which this information is to be gathered. She needs to follow that process closely if it is defined.

If the gathering method is not defined, suggest recording data on notecards. Using this approach, every source (book, magazine, person, etc.) should have a separate group of notecards held together with a rubber band. The top notecard in the group should contain the title, author, publisher, date of publication, or name of the person spoken to. Enter each fact gathered from the source on a *different* notecard with page references, including whether the information is a direct quote or a paraphrase. Also, briefly note the source on each card.

Step 3: Organizing

After the facts have been gathered, they need to be organized in a logical order. Now your child decides how the facts will be used. You can help her at this point by suggesting that she read her notes aloud to listen for different ideas. If she has developed a feeling for her topic and the various aspects of it, she should be able to understand how the different ideas relate to each other.

Each of the broad ideas or aspects of the topic should be listed and then arranged in an order that will allow your child to explain the topic in writing to someone who has no knowledge of it. This organization can be a formal outline (often required by teachers), or simply a list with supporting facts from the notes. This outline or list will guide your child through the orderly writing of the paper.

The last part of this step is to arrange all notecards into separate groups, each of which matches a subject area or idea in her list or outline.

Step 4: Talking on Paper

Once your child finishes steps 1–3, she has completed the research for her paper. She is now ready to begin writing. Research and organization are the key differences between the library paper and other writing assignments. If your child has spent sufficient time researching, discussing, and thinking about her topic, the actual writing should not be much different from other writing assignments.

So, the first step in writing is "talking on paper." Once again, getting those first words onto the page may be difficult, but you can remind her that this is not much different from other writing. She should know from experience that problems will be eliminated through the process of writing. Suggest that she move to her comfortable writing location and begin to write whatever comes into her mind about each aspect of the topic. Your comments at this point should include directions to follow her list or outline as she "talks" about the topic. Remind her to use her notes to supply the facts as she writes and to place each new idea in her outline or list into a new paragraph.

Step 5: Private Talking Out Loud

Your child should now read the first draft aloud, but to herself. She is her own first audience. Remind her that listening to her own voice inside her head will not work as well. This step should suggest what revisions should be made.

The Writing Tools

Library Paper Builder

Assignment: *Select an invention from the 20th century and describe its impact on society*

Step 1. Choosing My Topic (Check each step as it is completed.)
- ✓ I have read much about my topic from **3** sources. *(specify the number)*
- ✓ I have thought a great deal about my topic.
- ✓ I have discussed my topic with someone at home.
- ✓ I have discussed my topic with my teacher.
- ✓ I have made my topic very specific.
- ✓ I can find enough information about my topic for the requirements.
- ✓ I received approval for my topic from the teacher.

Step 2. Gathering (Check each step as it is completed.)
- ___ I am following the teacher's instructions for gathering my facts.
- ✓ I did not have note-gathering instructions and I am using note cards.
- ✓ I have a separate group of cards for every source.
- ✓ I have labeled the top note card of every group.
- ✓ I have put each fact on a different note card.
- ✓ I have labeled each note card with the page.
- ✓ I have labeled each note card as a direct quote or a paraphrase.
- ✓ I have briefly noted the source on each note card.

Step 3. Organizing (Check each step as it is completed.)
- ✓ I read my notes aloud.
- ✓ I listed all of my different ideas.
- ✓ I arranged the different ideas into a logical order.
- ___ I placed my different ideas into an outline.
- ✓ I placed my different ideas in order on one list.
- ✓ I arranged my note cards to match the order of my outline or list.

Step 4. Talking on Paper (Check each step as it is completed.)
- ✓ I found a comfortable place to write.
- ✓ I followed my list or outline as I wrote.
- ✓ I used my notes to find the facts as I wrote.
- ✓ I put each new idea into a new paragraph.

Library Paper Builder, *continued*

Step 5. Private Talking Out Loud (Check each step as it is completed.)
- ✓ I read my paper aloud to hear how it sounded.
- ✓ I changed the things that didn't sound right.

Step 6. Public Talking Out Loud (Check each step as it is completed.)
- ___ I asked at least one person to listen to my paper as I read it.
- ✓ I asked more than one person to listen to my paper as I read it.
- ✓ I learned how people felt about what I read.
- ✓ I did more thinking about my paper when people asked me questions.

Step 7. Cleaning (Check each step as it is completed.)
- ✓ I went back to my comfortable writing spot.
- ✓ I reread my paper and made changes.
- ✓ I went back to my original sources to get more information to explain a confusing part.
- ✓ I need to read my paper aloud to someone again; it still needs cleaning.
- ✓ I have finished cleaning.
- ✓ I like what I have written.

Step 8. Polishing (Check each step as it is completed.)
- ✓ I checked my spelling.
- ✓ I checked my sentences.
- ✓ I checked my grammar.
- ✓ I checked that I met all the requirements of the paper.
- ✓ I think my paper is polished.

Step 6: Public Talking Out Loud

This is the opportunity for the "public" audience: a family member, another relative, or even the teacher. At this point your child should be listening for the way someone reacts to what she has written, and she should be responding to, or thinking about, the questions that are asked. This allows her to do more thinking about her writing before the "cleaning" begins.

Step 7: Cleaning

Now your child can go back to her comfortable writing spot and begin the cleaning process. She will need to reread, cross out or delete as needed, reword, and perhaps refer to her notes or to the original sources for additional information to clarify any confusing parts. Remind her that every good writer does this cleaning; this step is what will make the difference between a good and a poor library paper.

Step 8: Polishing

In this last step, your child should look at the spelling, grammar, sentence structure, and physical requirements of the paper if they have been specified by the teacher. Recommend that she resolve any grammatical questions before submitting the final paper. Be sure that she proofreads her work.

The *Library Paper Builder* allows you to guide your child through what is often a confusing and disorganized process. Although the specifics will vary from class to class and from community to community, the *Library Paper Builder* is general enough to act as an overlay to teachers' more specific requirements.

Activities for Younger Children

Younger children in grades one to three are learning to write at the same time they are learning other language skills. Although they do not have some of the skills that one traditionally associates with writing, they do have the most important requirements—a voice and a point of view. Children of all ages have something to say about any number of topics.

Encourage your child to express those thoughts in writing, even though her spelling and grammar skills are not fully developed. This encouragement will help your child to feel comfortable communicating on paper. This comfort level will reinforce the writing instruction that she receives in school. Try these activities:

Ask your child to tell the rest of the family about a movie she has just seen. Suggest that she write about it and even illustrate her writing. Guide her through the steps in the *Writing Organizer*. The steps are appropriate at any level, and they lead your child easily through the writing process.

In a situation in which you are upset about your child's behavior and have sent her to her room, you can ask her to explain her point of view in writing. Writing about it helps your child to think about the situation and discuss it rationally.

If your family is fortunate enough to have a computer with a word processor, encourage your first- to third-grader to compose original stories, helping her read and follow the steps of the organizer just like the "big kids."

Children of this age have an almost unlimited number of things they want to talk about. The use of a computer and the *Writing Organizer* could result in a family newspaper with contributions from all family members. Copies could be made for relatives.

Chapter 5

The Analysis Tools

The Analysis Tools

If you do something that works well, you'll continue to do it. On the other hand, if you try something that doesn't work, you probably won't do it again because you don't want to keep making the same mistake. Analyzing the results of what you're doing is an important habit for everyone to cultivate.

This certainly applies to your child's learning. He needs to be able to understand what he has done correctly and what he has done incorrectly. Analysis of learning methods and performance reinforces good study habits and eliminates inefficiencies.

Athletes have learned the value of analyzing their performances. They know that every game or match has two outcomes. One is the result of the match—the score. The other is the record of their performance on training films that they watch repeatedly to help identify, analyze, and ultimately improve both their training methods and performance.

Think about studying for a test as training for a game or match. Your child studies the best he can. If that studying results in an excellent grade, then the training methods worked. But if that studying results in less than a satisfactory grade, the child needs to understand what parts of the training need to be improved so that the next "game" will result in a better score.

Not all learning methods are equally effective with all children. The results depend on your child's own set of skills, learning style, and ability to concentrate. Because of this, it is important to analyze the effectiveness of each learning method as you try it.

In all aspects of life, we human beings constantly analyze the effectiveness of the tools we use to survive. We learn quickly that if we spend too much money on one thing, we don't have enough for something else. In social situations, we learn what produces the reactions we want in others; your child, like all children, learns which techniques get your attention and which techniques don't. So we learn to make choices based on what is most effective for us. In other words, we figure out how to get what we want.

Understanding what works to produce effective learning and what doesn't is part of learning. Your child needs to know which study techniques are successful and which are not. The successful techniques need to be continued, and the ones that don't work need to be stopped. As obvious as this sounds, your child may not understand the process and therefore may not employ it. Most children can understand it once it's explained. It is your job to explain and demonstrate the analysis process and reinforce it at home so that your child can apply it to all future activities in and out of school.

In the school setting, analysis can be applied to a vast variety of situations:

Why did I fail my math test?

Why did I get a great score from just a little studying in spelling and such a low score from a lot of studying in math?

Why do I always do my history homework and always skip my science homework?

Why are my test grades so low when my project grades are so high?

Easy approaches to effective learning will escape your child, unless he learns to analyze his learning methods. Unless your child understands that everything does not work equally well, he will be unable to solve problems, especially if no one has ever shown him how to isolate a problem in search of a solution. When handling adversity becomes less emotional and more rational, problems become challenges, rather than defeaters.

Problem and Reason Analyzer

This tool relies on communication. As you discuss the school day with your child, you will listen for potential problem areas and address them before they become major problems. Even if you and your child do not arrive at a complete solution, the information gleaned from the discussions and analysis will be valuable in your conversations with the classroom teacher. You'll find a blank *Problem and Reason Analyzer* form in the Appendix.

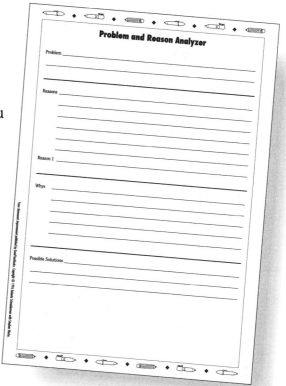

Here's how to use it:

Step 1: *Frequently* discuss the day, the class, the teacher, and the subject with your child. Ask how things are going in his different subjects, if he likes his teachers, if he understands what is being explored in each class, and if anything is really interesting, confusing, or boring.

You know your child better than anyone else. Therefore, you will know when things are less than perfect. Some typical symptoms of potential problems include anger while discussing the area, refusal to discuss it, tears, lying, and so forth. Use the *Problem and Reason Analyzer* in any area where you suspect a current or potential issue.

Step 2: Record your child's problem exactly as he stated it during your conversation. You should write it on the *Problem* line of the analyzer.

Step 3: *Discuss* (don't lecture) the issue with your child. Brainstorm by questioning and discussing the possible reasons for this problem. Your child may not wish to describe it as a problem. He may say that it is "No big deal." If he is reluctant, just agree that it really is no big deal, but if you don't talk about it, it will become one. As you brainstorm, jot down anything that strikes you as relevant or as a possible source of the problem. If information is not forthcoming, you might ask if your child is happy with the way things are and whether a solution would make him happier. If he can't identify possible reasons, ask him to guess at what might be happening. Another way to address an uncommunicative child is to project the situation onto someone else: If Johnny had the same problem, what would solve it for him? (This will remove any sense of personal failure from the discussion.) There are no right or wrong answers here. Instead, there are insights to the problem or issue and, along with those insights, possible solutions.

Step 4: List the reasons for the problem on the *Reasons* lines.

Step 5: Select the most important reason and list it on the line marked *Reason 1*.

Step 6: Analyze that reason and ask your child why that reason causes a problem. List all *Whys* for that reason on the appropriate lines.

Step 7: Look at the *Whys* with your child and list *Possible Solutions*.

Step 8: Help your child try to follow through on the potential solutions. Help your child assess the effectiveness of each solution. If a solution doesn't work, try the next one. If necessary, speak to your child's teacher about the problem. With the information supplied by the *Problem and Reason Analyzer*, your child's teacher will be able to help in solving the problem.

This approach to problem-solving will reduce your child's emotional response: no crying, no screaming, no failure, no ego-deflation. It will help him develop his ability to handle adversity in a rational and objective manner. Your child is learning how to solve problems—

not just school problems, but life problems. You have taught him that every problem has a solution, and that there is a method for finding that solution.

Activities for Younger Children

The *Problem and Reason Analyzer* works well with family issues. When an issue arises, use the analysis mode instead of shouting or punishing. Shouting and punishing often result in repetition of the same problem on another day. No lesson is learned and behaviors are not changed. The *Problem and Reason Analyzer* gives parents and children a way to step outside the problem and seek a solution together. The benefits are obvious: you are teaching your child the rudiments of conflict resolution as a solution to problems, as a replacement for the more impulsive behaviors of shouting, crying, or aggression.

Creating special "talking times" also is helpful—dinner, bedtime, Sunday evenings—setting aside a time for the family to get together to share concerns in a positive manner. Try to address a problem that arises during the week in one of these talking times.

Test Analysis Form

This tool is based on the idea that your child can use his old tests to do better on new ones. The *Test Analysis Form* lets you derive valuable information from completed tests. If your child understands why he lost points, study skills can be improved and good learning habits reinforced.

Very important: When examining completed tests, your attitude must be positive. The purpose of analyzing a test is to improve your child's performance on the next test, not to make him feel worse about errors on this one.

The Analysis Tools

> **Test Analysis Form**
>
> Course **History**
>
> ☑ Test
> ☐ Quiz
> **60** Grade
>
> **Analysis of Errors**
>
> **3, 16** Forgot to Study
> **8** Did Not Understand
> **7** Careless Mistake
> ___ Panic
> ___ Memory Loss

Here's how to use the *Test Analysis Forms* found in the *Appendix*:

Step 1: Examine the test with your child. Circle the numbers of the questions with errors.

Step 2: Discuss the reason for each error.

Step 3: With your child, find the reason on the *Test Analysis Form*.

Step 4: Place the number of each incorrectly answered question on the line opposite the corresponding reason.

Step 5: When finished, keep the labeled test in a *Test Analysis* folder so your child can examine it when he studies for the next test in that subject.

You can imagine the kinds of constructive conversations you and your child might have about old tests. As you analyze errors, you reinforce good learning habits.

Add Your Own Tools

Chapter 6

Add Your Own Tools

This chapter contains a multitude of ideas for you to use as tools toward expanding your child's learning potential. You can use all of the tools in this book as they have been presented, use them alone, or combine them in new and different ways as your child's learning needs dictate. As she expands her learning repertoire, she will become more flexible, creative, and active in her learning.

Mnemonics

We live in a complex world with a multitude of things to remember. Most of us use mnemonics every day, even though we may not be aware of it. For example, if you parked your car in row B4 at the mall and need to remember it, you might make up a mnemonic such as "B4 I panic, I should look in row B4."

Why not teach your child to create mnemonics when she tackles difficult material? This approach can work magic!

For example, if your child has repeated trouble spelling the word *arithmetic,* perhaps a mnemonic device would help:

A Rat In Tom's House May Eat The Ice Cream

A R I T H M E T I C

What child would forget how to spell arithmetic after learning this great mnemonic! Of course you wouldn't use something like this for every spelling word, only the ones that cause consistent problems.

Use this approach for problem situations and have fun with it. Be creative and draw from something that is meaningful to your child. Mnemonics make learning fun, and you will be teaching your child to create them by herself.

Here's how to create a mnemonic:

Write out the letters in a problem spelling, the first letters of the most important words in a series of steps, or the letters that represent the series to be memorized.

Think of words that start with each letter.

Tie the words together into a "silly" sentence.

Let's try more mnemonics. Has your child ever become confused when trying to determine if she should multiply or divide when converting standard measurements—inches to feet, pints to gallons, and so forth? This is a common problem for many children.

Here are two typical fourth-grade problems:

How many inches are there in 5 feet?

How many feet are there in 48 inches?

Add Your Own Tools

The teacher carefully explains that when changing from smaller units to larger units you divide the smaller units into the larger units. In spite of the careful explanation, your child still can't quite remember it.

You can turn the potentially frustrating situation into a fun problem using a mnemonic device. Instead of trying to remember "smaller to larger divide," you suggest:

Smaller to Larger	Divide
S L	D
Some Ladies	Dance

Some Ladies Dance! You have retained the important initial letters and your child knows what they stand for. She now has a funny way to remember the formula.

You need not develop a mnemonic for the opposite calculation (multiply to convert larger units to smaller units). Your child will remember "larger to smaller multiply" (LSM) as being the opposite of "Some Ladies Dance," because multiply is the opposite of divide.

How might your child use this approach to actually complete an arithmetic assignment?

5 feet = ? inches

48 inches = ? feet

Remembering "Some Ladies Dance," your child would write SLD on the paper and its opposite LSM. Now she knows when to divide and when to multiply. She won't become confused, because she knows what the letters mean.

She knows that

12 inches = 1 foot

so in solving the problem

48 inches = ? feet

she knows to use the number 12. But what should she do? The mnemonic reminds her that to go from

Smaller to Larger, she should Divide.

She divides the smaller units—the inches—by 12 and gets the answer.

48 inches ÷ 12 = 4 feet

Using the opposite mnemonic will help her to solve the other problem—converting larger units to smaller units. Since SLD results in division to convert from smaller to larger units, multiplication has to be used for converting in the opposite direction.

Your child knows that

12 inches = 1 foot

Add Your Own Tools

so in solving the problem

5 feet = ? inches

she knows to multiply the larger units (feet) by 12 to get the number of smaller units.

5 feet x 12 = 60 inches

For some children, this method almost works miracles. They don't have to worry if they forget the rule or become confused because they can rely on a mnemonic device such as "Some Ladies Dance." Math can be fun and creative for your child if you can turn a frustrating concept into a clever mnemonic.

The challenge of conversion between decimals and percents presents another ideal situation for applying this method. The basic concept is moving the decimal two places, but whether to move it to the left or the right often causes panic at test time.

Here's the rule: when changing from *percent* to *decimal,* move the decimal point two places to the *left*.

Build your mnemonic from the key words (italicized above). P D L could become "Please Don't Litter."

Your child can now easily solve problems such as:

625% = ? decimal

PDL reminds your child to move the decimal point to the left if she is converting from a percent to a decimal. She can answer the problem in a flash!

625% = 6.25

Based on the mnemonic, your child will also be able to puzzle through the opposite conversion: decimal to percent moves the decimal point right. Since PDL moves the decimal point to the left, the opposite situation moves it to the right.

Here's one more mnemonic for math. Does your child get confused when asked to read large numbers? Lots of adults would rather not read this number: 125,000,000,000,000,000 (one hundred twenty five quadrillion). How do you know what number it is?

Try this: He Told Me Better Talk Quietly

Moving from right to left, the initial letters of the place values are shown under each group of three digits:

Mnemonic devices can be extremely helpful in problem situations. But don't use them unless there is a problem. Too many can be confusing.

Children understand the usefulness of mnemonics. So in a problem learning situation, you won't have to create the mnemonic. All you have to do is to suggest that she develop one. She will know how.

Activities for Younger Children

Mnemonics are fun for little kids as well. They enjoy both making them up and being able to remember their meaning. It generates a great sense of accomplishment.

You can give your younger child that sense of accomplishment by applying mnemonics to her life as well as to school. Try one of these:

> When you are food shopping one day, ask her to get four or five things for you and to use a mnemonic to remember all of them.

> Give your child four or five tasks to finish in your home within the next two or three days to demonstrate that a mnemonic is durable—it can jog her memory even days later.

> If your child likes sports, try developing a pattern that will name all the teams in a league, the starting lineup of a favorite team, or all the kids in a karate class or on a soccer team. This fun-filled exercise will instill the concept.

> Don't forget to help your child develop a mnemonic for that difficult spelling word.

▶ **Add Your Own Tools**

Colors

Students are always being asked to learn associations—between words and parts of speech, wars with battles, presidents with political parties, and so forth. Some associative learning tools have already been covered; here are a few more.

Research suggests that color can help separate groups by providing a physical way to distinguish abstract concepts. To use colored paper to learn associations:

> Organize any facts to be learned according to their categories.
>
> Select one color for each category.
>
> Write each fact on the correct paper color.
>
> Study the facts using any of the tools in the *Practice Tool,* Chapter 3.

Memory of the color can help to trigger memory of the facts written on that color and, therefore, of the category in which those facts belong.

Red Paper

Vitamin B
- Known as thiamin
- Found in yeast, liver, nuts, pork, and whole grain cereals
- Lack of this vitamin could result in beriberi

Yellow Paper

Vitamin A
- Known as the anti-infection vitamin
- Found in butter, eggs, and fish liver oils
- Lack of this vitamin may result in a kind of blindness

Green Paper

Vitamin C
- Known as the anti-scurvy vitamin
- Found in fresh fruits, vegetables, and meat
- Lack of this vitamin could result in scurvy

Color can also be helpful when making *Flash Cards*. For example, if your child needs to learn the part of speech for each of several words, use color: put all nouns on white cards, verbs on yellow, and so forth.

Encourage your child's creativity in using this tool. Its applications to schoolwork are endless. Color makes all kinds of learning easier.

Paper, Pens, and Pencils

The kinds of paper, pens, and pencils that your child uses can actually affect her success in school because incorrect tools can interfere with her ability to demonstrate what she has learned. Children oftentimes are drawn to the latest craze in school supplies. In fact, you may be drawn to the items that are least expensive. However, learning style is more important than either one. You need to purchase items that are *right* for your child. Here are some examples.

Some kids have difficulty writing their math examples on a piece of paper. Their numbers may not align and the examples lack organization on the page. If you recognize this difficulty in your own child, why not try graph paper for all math work?

For writing assignments, the width of the lines on your child's paper may not match her motor skill development. If they are too wide and provide space that your child no longer needs, she will be unhappy with her composition's appearance. Lines that are too narrow don't provide enough space for a child whose fine motor skills are not as well developed; she will be frustrated by her inability to use the space provided. Both situations interfere with your child's ability to demonstrate her learning.

Children who are pleased with how their written work looks on paper are more likely to do that work. Experiment with the kind of paper your child uses. If necessary, try all kinds until you find one that seems to work best.

What about writing tools? Children need to feel comfortable with their writing tools. The writing tool needs to match the child's motor skills development level.

Some children can't write with certain shapes and sizes of pencils or pens. These writing instruments present difficulty because of the control required to manipulate them:

- ◆ Lead that's too hard or sharp for a child will frequently break.
- ◆ A fine-point pen may be too delicate for a child who can't control pressure, and its use will result in messy papers.
- ◆ A pen point that is too hard may cause fatigue after short periods of writing.
- ◆ Pencils with flattened sides will promote correct finger positioning.

- Pens that have rubberized or high-friction surfaces will prevent slipping.
- Felt-tip pens may help to prevent fatigue.

Go to the store and try a variety of pens with your child until she finds one with which she is comfortable.

Before adults make decisions, they spend some time considering which choice is best. Try offering your child the same opportunity.

Colored Pens and Highlighters

The use of color in notetaking can help some students retain information.

Have your child try these easy study aids. When studying a foreign language, underline (or write) all the masculine words in blue and all the feminine words in red. When studying the strengths and weaknesses of the North and South during the Civil War, write the North's strengths in blue and the South's in red. Highlight class notes for vocabulary words, characters in a book, or identifications in social studies.

Encourage your child to be creative. The applications are endless!

Word Associations

Good memory enhances learning. Children blessed with good memories frequently experience less stressful learning. This section is appropriate if your child seems to have a poor memory, or if you just don't know her memory abilities. Some children who demonstrate memory "problems" may not have poor memories at all; they simply may not be planning to remember.

Add Your Own Tools

Word associations are another way to deal with the "unknowns" identified by using the tools in Chapter 3 *The Practice Tool: Flash Cards, Matching Decks, Sorting Boxes,* and *Four-Column Pages.*

Foreign language study provides a good example of how word associations can work. Here is a typical list of French vocabulary words entered on *Split Sheets* (see Chapter 3).

Split Sheets

Word	Association
dormir	to sleep
camera	camera
anthropophage	cannibal
faire l'appoint	to have the right change
avoir du nerf	to have nerves of steel

The first and easiest association is between those words that are the same or similar in English.

camera	camera

This can eliminate many words on a list. It may seem obvious to you and ridiculous to point out to your child, but assume nothing. What is obvious to an adult is not always obvious to a child.

Add Your Own Tools

The next most obvious association on this list would link *dormir* to its meaning "to sleep" by using the association—to sleep in a *dorm*itory.

| dormir | to sleep |

For difficult associations, those without an obvious link, encourage your child to invent wild associations using her imagination. The more unusual the association, the more likely it is to be remembered at test time.

How about this one for

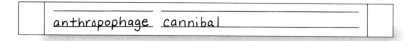

AN ANT WAS THROWN in a CAGE because there was a CANNIBAL eating the other ants.

It's farfetched; it might work for your child or it might not. Everyone's different. Make up your own association for these words. You can help your child with the associations she can't make alone, but you'll be surprised at how quickly she will be using this method and how rarely you'll have to assist.

Consider this for the next difficult association.

How about:

| faire l'appoint | to have the right change |

I APPOINT you to have the right change (FARE) every time we use the bus.

| avoir du nerf | to have nerves of steel |

think of Nerf® balls being thrown. You don't need TO HAVE NERVES OF STEEL to catch a Nerf® ball.

Try it with your child. You can even challenge the whole family to help with difficult associations.

Corrected Homework

Your child's homework is a valuable study aid for the next quiz or test! *Don't let it be thrown away without serving its full purpose!* Wastebaskets at home and school are full of homework papers that have been tossed because students thought they were of no further use. This could not be further from the truth.

Math, science, and grammar homework, especially, may fall into this category because this homework is usually assigned to reinforce or practice concepts—concepts that are highly likely to appear in future testing. This type of homework is often self-corrected in class, allowing your child to ask questions. During this process, most children pay attention, nod that they now understand, and even make corrections on their homework paper. Then they throw it away.

What a waste! All that hard work is lost. These papers contain the concepts your child understood and the ones she had difficulty understanding. This resource should be used in studying.

Here's how to use corrected homework:

At test and quiz time, or when your child has no homework and you wish that she did, have her redo all the problem concepts.

Have her work on problem areas. If difficulty continues, you will know exactly which concepts will be difficult for your child in the future.

Guide your child to address the specific problem areas: an after-school session with the teacher might be requested to reinforce or reteach the difficult concepts.

The benefits of using corrected homework are:

- ◆ You don't have to quiz your child at test time.
- ◆ The problem areas have been identified and therefore can be addressed.
- ◆ A phone call to school can alert the teacher to the problem concept that needs review. (Kids don't usually want to ask for help.)
- ◆ You have guided your child to address concepts not easily grasped and to persevere until mastery.

A child who understands that learning involves mastery of difficult concepts—not just the easy ones—and who knows how to address those difficulties is well on the way to mastery learning. This is what you want for your child. Half learning or poorly understanding difficult concepts will result in school problems and a weak foundation on which to build new learning.

This is not a punishment for poor homework, so don't get carried away. You are trying to instill a positive attitude about learning. That won't happen if a frustrating day at school is followed by an evening of more frustration. Be positive and encouraging, praise all efforts, and start *slowly*.

Guess the Test

Believe it or not, using *Guess the Test* can bring your child as close as possible to looking forward to a test as she discovers how much she can learn about the test before it actually occurs!

Guess the Test establishes the content of the test before studying. It eliminates the study of unimportant information and suggests the appropriate method of studying.

Here's how to use Guess the Test:

Have your child look at old tests and guess at the possible format for the upcoming test based on what the teacher has done in the past.

Review homework, class discussions, papers, and projects to guess what the test will require.

Make a list of the concepts likely to be covered.

Have your child ask her teacher about the test. Here are some areas to investigate:

- ◆ Will it be objective (true/false), fill-in-the-blank, or multiple choice? Will there be essay questions?
- ◆ Will she be expected to give her opinion, prove a point, or compare and contrast?

- Will she be expected to solve a problem using one of several new approaches?
- Will she be expected to construct something to demonstrate that she understands?

These kinds of questions will provide your child with the information she needs to study the correct material efficiently in the appropriate format.

Introduction of *Guess the Test* when children are young (and when tests and quizzes are not complex) will make them increasingly comfortable about asking the appropriate questions as test complexity increases. It is easy to train a child to think about a test as more than just an evaluation of her knowledge. Once your child gets into the habit of guessing what will be on the test in an organized way, she can create practice tests and study with them. Your child will be actively learning.

When your child starts playing *Guess the Test*, she will not be batting a thousand. With practice, however, her guesses at test content will improve. As this happens, your child will begin to "guess the test" instinctively, and your role as a facilitator will diminish.

Sneak-a-Peek Sheets

Sneak-a-Peek Sheets eliminate much of the anxiety at test time that produces poor results.

Other tools suggested throughout this book involve creating lists, charts, mnemonics and letter patterns, color-coded pairs of items, and so on. These are essentially *mind pictures* that your child can call upon at test time. Anxiety at test time, however, may block the use of these mind pictures. Things easily remembered during studying can disappear during a test when anxiety is a factor. This anxiety is self-fueling and multiplies as the student looks at the test and self-doubts begin to build:

> "Oh, no! I didn't expect that on the test!"

> "I can't remember that!"

> "I'll never have time to do that!"

In these anxious moments, some children easily forget the lists, charts, and patterns they need to demonstrate their understanding.

Children love the *Sneak-a-Peek Sheets* idea. It's obvious, yet very few kids ever think of using it "legally." You can easily and quickly introduce this concept, monitor its use, and watch your child enter the testing situation with increased confidence.

Add Your Own Tools

Here's how it works:

In the classroom, have your child ask for a blank piece of paper *before* she reads the test.

She then jots down all the charts, key words, and so on that she developed during study time.

Then, as she takes the test, she can refer to all her charts, notes, and outlines. She doesn't get confused and doesn't worry about getting confused. There's no concern about forgetting, and she remains calm.

Most kids would never think of doing this "legally." You must encourage your child to do it. When this technique is suggested, more than one child has looked at the teacher or parent incredulously and asked, "Isn't that cheating?" The answer is "Definitely not." Bringing information to a test in one's mind is not cheating. Putting it on paper merely eliminates the chance of forgetting it. This is smart test taking.

The Testing Issue

Regardless of what it is called (some schools call it *testing,* others call it *assessment*), the evaluation of what your child has learned is an essential element of the educational experience. In the past, objective testing was used most frequently with essay questions added occasionally.

Today, however, testing philosophy is moving away from using the "one right answer" format, because this approach often tests only fragmented and isolated pieces of information. Instead, testing is moving toward the evaluation of how well students can integrate and apply what they know in real-life situations.

Your child may be in one of the many classrooms where this newer approach is part of everyday learning, or your child may be in a school using the more traditional testing modes.

Although much of the information in this book addresses performance on objective kinds of tests, the techniques suggested here can also be applied in schools that subscribe to the newer philosophy of testing. Good teachers have always combined both approaches to assess children. What is different in many communities is the emphasis on introducing real-life assessments in classrooms where they did not exist.

What does this mean to you and your child? If your child is in a school that asks students to demonstrate knowledge in real-life situations, your parental role is even more important. Use real-life situations to help her practice what she has learned. This requires a working knowledge of what she is learning at school, which you will have automatically if you follow the processes in this book.

Consider these guidelines and examples of using real-life situations:

Mathematics

Your child needs to know what tools to use to solve a problem. Will she need to use a paper and pencil, a calculator, an estimation, or can she solve it "in her head"? She may need to make sketches or give brief explanations to support her solutions to problems. The more she practices this type of activity, the sharper she will be at this type of thinking.

Try these to develop your child's facility with numbers.

- On your next trip to the food store, ask her to estimate the cost of your groceries. This will take some practice, but you will be surprised at how quickly the estimate will begin to approximate the actual cost.

- Next time you fill your car's gas tank, ask your child to calculate how many miles you got to the gallon. Ask her to estimate mileage economy in city and open highway driving.

- If you are fortunate enough to have a computer with a spreadsheet program or software that manages your finances, encourage your child to examine her own finances (allowance, gifts, even "pretend" investments she might make).

- Open a savings account for your child and ask her to estimate the interest and the future balances as she develops a savings plan.

- Ask her to track finances on a day trip or an extended vacation using a calculator. Ask her to record the information in any way that makes sense to her and then ask her to explain it.

Reading

Your child will be asked to interpret what she reads in addition to demonstrating an understanding of what she reads. Some questions will focus on general comprehension of the material. Others do not have right or wrong answers and depend, instead, upon the child's interpretation and her ability to support her answer with specific information from the reading.

Try these activities to develop the ability to form opinions on reading material.

- Read a story to several gathered family members, or have more than one person in the family read the same story. Then have a discussion about a character in the story. The discussion should focus on opinions, not on questions with right or wrong answers. The rules of your discussion, however, need to require that all statements about the character be backed up by evidence from the story. For instance:

Did the character make the correct choice, and why do you feel that way?

What other choice could the character have made at a crucial point in the story?

Keep the discussion lively!

- The next time your child reads an assigned book, ask her to explain the story to you. Then ask:

    How it is similar to or different from other books she's read?

    Did she learn a new idea from reading the book?

    Can she predict what will happen if a sequel for the book is written?

- Use television shows or movies in the same way as you would use a book to help your child discuss open-ended questions.

- Visit the library or bookstore with your child to select books related to something in which she has an interest. Encourage her to learn more about the subject no matter what the topic. If it's a subject of interest, it's a valid one to explore at the library or bookstore. Don't insist on a subject related to school.

- Encourage your child to read any item of interest from the daily newspaper and to discuss it with the family at mealtime. Make the discussion lively by encouraging family members to offer their opinions. Remember to request facts to support opinions.

Writing

Your child is asked to write for different purposes. She might be writing to inform someone about a particular subject or experience, to persuade someone to agree with her, or to compose a story or other original work. The goal is to communicate a message using the written word. This practice can be fun.

Try these exercises to develop your child's ability to express her thoughts in writing.

- Encourage your child to keep a journal where she can record her reactions, thoughts, and questions about daily events.

- The next time your child asks you for something that you are not inclined to allow, ask her to persuade you in writing.

Add Your Own Tools

- If you and your child disagree about an issue, rather than fighting about it, try writing about it. Suggest that both of you exchange letters that explain the issue as each of you sees it. You will be surprised at how "civilized" your disagreements will become and how adult your child's explanation will be.

- Once again, if you have a computer at home with a word-processing program, encourage your child to use it for creative writing. Suggest that she develop some ideas in her journal into a story. Using some of the new computer applications, she could even illustrate her story. Encourage her to clean and polish her story and then print it for others to enjoy.

- If your child has a strong opinion about a local issue in the community or at school, suggest that she express that opinion in writing—perhaps as a letter to the editor of your newspaper.

Today's testing methods may be different from those that you experienced. However, if you encourage your child to use her skills and knowledge in real-life situations, you will be providing the home support necessary to help your child succeed to the very best of her ability.

Music, Music, Music

Have you ever wondered how children can remember all the words to a song and yet are unable to remember number facts, multiplication tables, or any sequenced learning task? Why not capture your child's natural ability with music and apply it to learning!

Try this:

- Select a favorite tune and change the words to accommodate the series to be learned.
- Then, sing it together and record it on a tape recorder.
- Have your child sing along while listening.

The pattern created by the song automatically places any element in the series. When your child is unable to remember an element, all she needs to do is find the correct spot in the song. There are many songs that you can use to remember a series of elements. "The Alphabet Song" is one of the best known.

Think about all the music in your child's life and how you can tap it for learning needs. This makes learning fun, both for the child and for the family. Try to sing the songs in the car, and have your child entertain you and her grandparents, for example.

 **Add Your Own Tools**

Tape Recorder Magic

Is your child using a tape recorder while studying? Almost every home has one, and yet few children use them for studying. The applications are numerous, limited only by the imagination.

Here's how to use a tape recorder for spelling:

- ◆ You or your child pronounce the word into the recorder.
- ◆ Wait a few seconds.
- ◆ Spell the word.
- ◆ At study time have your child listen to the words on tape and then write the word during the few seconds of silence (or shut off the tape if more time is needed).
- ◆ She can play the tape again to hear the correct spelling and check her answer against the tape.

This is a great tool for a child who learns best when listening. It frees you from quizzing your child, it allows your child to demonstrate her knowledge in a form that will be requested during the test, and it is multisensory in its approach: Hear it! Write it! See it!

This technique can be applied in such areas as the study of languages, where students are expected to communicate orally. Suggest that your child practice her new language skills by using the tape recorder to discuss everyday issues. She can then bring the tape to school for the teacher's response, or share it with another speaker who is more proficient in the language. Oral language proficiency comes with practice, and the tape recorder is the perfect tool for this.

A child who has learned to use the tape recorder as a study tool in the earlier grades will turn to its use when study demands increase in high school. An added benefit is that the tape recorder can be used anywhere: studying can be done in the park, on a bus, or while riding in the car.

The tape recorder can be used for writing assignments by children who are able to speak more effectively than they can write. Your child should organize her writing using the *Writing Organizer* (Chapter 4), and speak her composition into the tape. Then have her play it back and write what she hears.

A tape recorder can be useful for children facing a variety of learning challenges. Experiment with its use in different areas to discover what works.

Taking Words/Getting Questions

The inability to take notes is a widespread problem among students in higher grades. This skill is necessary for student survival. You can develop this important skill by helping your child to learn how to take notes in the early grades.

Learning to take good notes yields several benefits:

- ◆ It gives the student information about what the teacher considers important and therefore what is likely to appear on tests.

- ◆ It allows your child to practice notetaking when it may not be necessary. You have given your child an important skill for later use and encouraged her to practice it now.

- ◆ It encourages purposeful listening and concentration, possibly the least recognized benefit of acquiring this skill early on.

Inability to concentrate is a major issue for students. An older student who has this difficulty misses valuable information that may not be repeated. Children with wandering minds are likely to have low grades. Yet allowing the mind to wander may be a habit acquired at a young age and never broken. Training your child's mind to concentrate is worth the effort.

Here are steps for taking "listening" notes:

- ◆ Tell your child to jot down words or phrases, *not sentences*, when she hears something important.

- ◆ Your child should leave lots of space on the paper where she misses something.

- ◆ At home that night, jog her memory by using her listening "words."

- ◆ Read each word aloud and ask her to elaborate.

- ◆ She can add any additional information she remembers to her notes in the blank spaces.

Your child will usually be able to supply much of the omitted information because it will be stored in her short-term memory. Much of the missing information may be what she was unable to record quickly enough, but some may in fact represent concepts she did not understand and passed over. If she can identify this situation, the information may be accessed by contacting another student in the class or by asking the teacher specific questions about it the next day.

An efficient form for note-taking is the "Main Idea/Detail" format. In this format, your child's words or phrases become the main ideas. The information your child is able to provide during elaboration supplies the details.

Main Idea
    Detail
    Detail

Main Idea
    Detail
    Detail

Add Your Own Tools

Transportation Inventions

Kinds
  Automobile
  Airship
  Airplane

Automobile
  Europeans invented it
  Rich 1st owners
  1900 — 1800+ in U.S.
  Benefits
    faster than a bike
    carried more people than bikes

Airplanes
  Invented by Orville and Wilbur Wright
    Interested in planes
    owned a bike shop
    Built planes with gas engines
  Orville
    Flew a plane on Dec. 17, 1903, at Kitty Hawk
    plane in air for 12 sec.

Airships
  Experiments in U.S. and Europe
  Developed in 1800 by the French
  Made from huge balloons
    filled with gas
    engines
    propellers

Today
  All are still used

Consider this example of note-taking on the subject of transportation inventions, using this format.

Add Your Own Tools

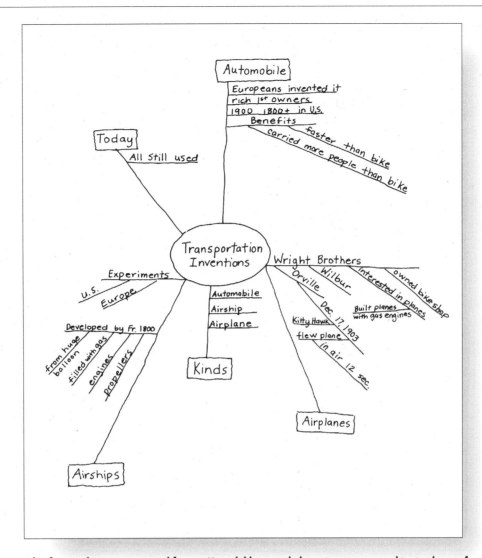

Here is an example of note-taking using a visual format. Your child can study by trying to re-create his visual notes from memory.

At test time, encourage your child to use notes to help her study. Your child can look at the *Main Idea* (with details covered of course) and turn it into a question. Answering the question allows her to study independently. You don't have to quiz her. She is using listening notes to prepare for a class test. The auditory learner and the child who benefits from a multisensory approach (and most children do) would also do well to speak the answers at the same time she is writing them.

Another way of organizing class notes arranges the main idea and its details more visually. Teachers sometimes give information about an idea and then connect it to what seems like an unrelated story. Then, when students try to return to their notes, they are lost because the structure and focus of the topic have changed.

Students who feel comfortable taking notes in a more visual pattern will have much less difficulty relating the facts to the topic at the correct point on their page of notes. This is helpful if your child is trying to take notes from a lecture that is not arranged in a specific sequence.

Chapter 7

The End and the Beginning

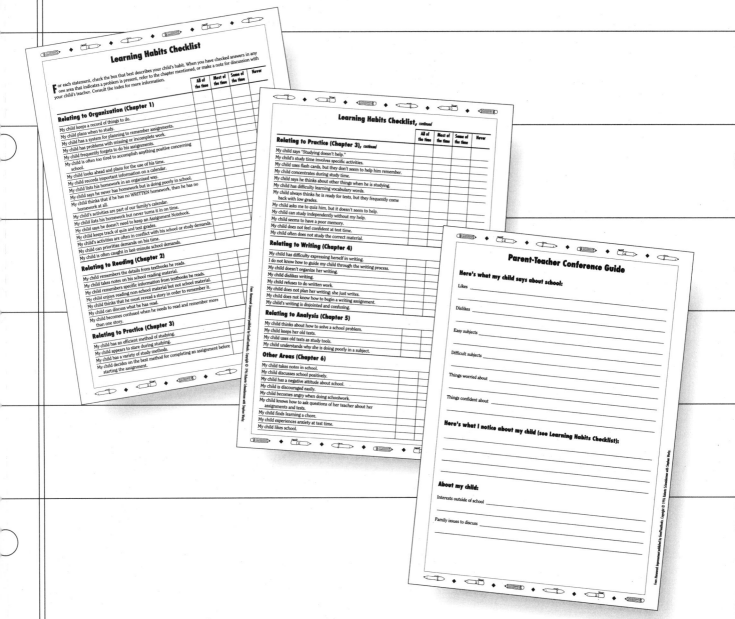

The End and the Beginning

The tools in this book empower you to make a difference in your child's education. You have the skills to help your child become everything she can become. You can make a difference in how much and how well your child achieves in school and in life.

You are communicating high expectations when you assist your child by the methods suggested in *Homework Improvement*. No one can do it for you, and no one can do it as well. You, your child, the school, and this book are an unbeatable team.

Remember not to try all the tools at once. You will become discouraged as your child becomes overwhelmed. First try the tools that make the most sense for your child. Introduce them one at a time until they become easy, natural parts of everyday school life.

Use the *Learning Habits Checklist* in the *Appendix* to discover the areas in which your child may need assistance. Once you have identified the areas, use the tools most relevant to that area. Once you have started using the tools in this book, reassess your child's needs two or three times each school year. This will allow you to change focus if necessary.

As your child adapts and becomes accustomed to these techniques, introduce additional tools to address current learning demands. A very young child may use only a few tools, an older child, many. The best part is that your role decreases as your child's skills increase.

Record your assessment on the *Parent Teacher Conference Guide*. This guide, combining information from the *Learning Habits Checklist* with other information about your child's attitudes towards school, will make your meeting with your child's teacher direct, efficient, and—most important—specific to your child's needs. The information you bring to the conference can be combined with the teacher's observations to form a complete profile of your child. As a team, you can work together to create solutions for any problem areas.

It's a good idea to keep the *Parent Teacher Conference Guide* handy so that you can accumulate your observations over time. The form will work best if you don't wait until the night before the meeting to fill it in. It may be wise to request an appointment prior to a scheduled conference if the nature of the information on your *Parent Teacher Conference Guide* concerns you. If you don't have time to attend a conference, call the teacher to explain that you will be sending this form and to arrange a telephone conference with feedback.

When you, your child, and the teacher are working together using the tools in *Homework Improvement,* you will be a parent who is guiding your child's learning in the best possible way. You will be able to rate yourself positively on all of these statements:

- I know what my child is studying in school.
- I am in regular communication with my child's teachers.
- I am confident that I can help my child learn in the correct way.
- I know how to direct my child to success in school.
- My child and I work calmly together on school related issues.
- I have enough time to help my child.
- I spend less money on unnecessary school supplies than I did a year ago.
- My child and I discuss schoolwork.

- My child is proud of her grades.
- I know how to explain my child's school problem to her teacher.
- Report cards do not contain surprises.

Congratulations! You have found the path to helping your child reach full learning potential. Stick to it! Those children who have the tools to succeed have a strong advantage throughout their school careers and, most importantly, throughout their lives.

Appendix

Learning Habits Checklist

Parent-Teacher Conference Guide

Daily Assignment Planner

Monthly Calendar

Weekly Schedule

Read It and Own It

Story Analyzer

Flash Cards

Matching Deck

Sorting Box

Split Sheet

Four-Column Page

Puzzle Chart

Writing Organizer

Library Paper Builder

Problem and Reason Analyzer

Test Analysis Form

Learning Habits Checklist

For each statement, check the box that best describes your child's habit. When you have checked answers in any one area that indicates a problem is present, refer to the chapter mentioned, or make a note for discussion with your child's teacher. Consult the index for more information.

Relating to Organization (Chapter 1)

	All of the time	Most of the time	Some of the time	Never
My child keeps a record of things to do.				
My child plans when to study.				
My child has a system for planning to remember assignments.				
My child has problems with missing or incomplete work.				
My child frequently forgets to do his assignments.				
My child is often too tired to accomplish anything positive concerning school.				
My child looks ahead and plans for the use of his time.				
My child records important information on a calendar.				
My child lists his homework in an organized way.				
My child says he never has homework but is doing poorly in school.				
My child thinks that if he has no WRITTEN homework, then he has no homework at all.				
My child's activities are part of our family's calendar.				
My child lists his homework but never turns it in on time.				
My child says he doesn't need to keep an Assignment Notebook.				
My child keeps track of quiz and test grades.				
My child's activities are often in conflict with his school or study demands.				
My child can prioritize demands on his time.				
My child is often caught in last-minute school demands.				

Relating to Reading (Chapter 2)

My child remembers the details from textbooks he reads.				
My child takes notes on his school reading material.				
My child remembers specific information from textbooks he reads.				
My child enjoys reading non-school material but not school material.				
My child thinks that he must reread a story in order to remember it.				
My child can discuss what he has read.				
My child becomes confused when he needs to read and remember more than one story.				

Relating to Practice (Chapter 3)

My child has an efficient method of studying.				
My child appears to stare during studying.				
My child has a variety of study methods.				
My child decides on the best method for completing an assignment before starting the assignment.				

Learning Habits Checklist, continued

	All of the time	Most of the time	Some of the time	Never
Relating to Practice (Chapter 3), continued				
My child says "Studying doesn't help."				
My child's study time involves specific activities.				
My child uses flash cards, but they don't seem to help him remember.				
My child concentrates during study time.				
My child says he thinks about other things when he is studying.				
My child has difficulty learning vocabulary words.				
My child always thinks he is ready for tests, but they frequently come back with low grades.				
My child asks me to quiz him, but it doesn't seem to help.				
My child can study independently without my help.				
My child seems to have a poor memory.				
My child does not feel confident at test time.				
My child often does not study the correct material.				
Relating to Writing (Chapter 4)				
My child has difficulty expressing herself in writing.				
I do not know how to guide my child through the writing process.				
My child doesn't organize her writing.				
My child dislikes writing.				
My child refuses to do written work.				
My child does not plan her writing; she just writes.				
My child does not know how to begin a writing assignment.				
My child's writing is disjointed and confusing.				
Relating to Analysis (Chapter 5)				
My child thinks about how to solve a school problem.				
My child keeps her old tests.				
My child uses old tests as study tools.				
My child understands why she is doing poorly in a subject.				
Other Areas (Chapter 6)				
My child takes notes in school.				
My child discusses school positively.				
My child has a negative attitude about school.				
My child is discouraged easily.				
My child becomes angry when doing schoolwork.				
My child knows how to ask questions of her teacher about her assignments and tests.				
My child finds learning a chore.				
My child experiences anxiety at test time.				
My child likes school.				

Parent-Teacher Conference Guide

Here's what my child says about school:

Likes _____
_____

Dislikes _____
_____

Easy subjects _____
_____

Difficult subjects _____
_____

Things worried about _____
_____

Things confident about _____
_____

Here's what I notice about my child (see Learning Habits Checklist):

_____
_____
_____
_____

About my child:

Interests outside of school _____
_____

Family issues to discuss _____
_____

Daily Assignment Planner

Day _____ Date _____

H	Assignments	T	Due Date

Daily Assignment Planner

Day _____ Date _____

H	Assignments	T	Due Date

From Homework Improvement published by GoodYearBooks. Copyright © 1996 Roberta Schneiderman with Stephen Werby.

Daily Assignment Planner

Grades _____ Term _____ Semester _____

Class			
	Tests	Quizzes	Homework/Classwork

Class			
	Tests	Quizzes	Homework/Classwork

Class			
	Tests	Quizzes	Homework/Classwork

Class			
	Tests	Quizzes	Homework/Classwork

Daily Assignment Planner

Grades _____ Term _____ Semester _____

Class			
	Tests	Quizzes	Homework/Classwork

Class			
	Tests	Quizzes	Homework/Classwork

Class			
	Tests	Quizzes	Homework/Classwork

Class			
	Tests	Quizzes	Homework/Classwork

From *Homework Improvement* published by GoodYearBooks. Copyright © 1996 Roberta Schneideman with Stephen Werby.

Monthly Calendar

Month _____   Year _____

Sunday	Monday	Tuesday	Wednesday	Thursday	Friday	Saturday

Weekly Schedule

Week of _____ To _____

Monday	Tuesday	Wednesday	Thursday	Friday	Saturday	Sunday
2:00 ___	2:00 ___	2:00 ___	2:00 ___	2:00 ___	2:00 ___	2:00 ___
2:30 ___	2:30 ___	2:30 ___	2:30 ___	2:30 ___	2:30 ___	2:30 ___
3:00 ___	3:00 ___	3:00 ___	3:00 ___	3:00 ___	3:00 ___	3:00 ___
3:30 ___	3:30 ___	3:30 ___	3:30 ___	3:30 ___	3:30 ___	3:30 ___
4:00 ___	4:00 ___	4:00 ___	4:00 ___	4:00 ___	4:00 ___	4:00 ___
4:30 ___	4:30 ___	4:30 ___	4:30 ___	4:30 ___	4:30 ___	4:30 ___
5:00 ___	5:00 ___	5:00 ___	5:00 ___	5:00 ___	5:00 ___	5:00 ___
5:30 ___	5:30 ___	5:30 ___	5:30 ___	5:30 ___	5:30 ___	5:30 ___
6:00 ___	6:00 ___	6:00 ___	6:00 ___	6:00 ___	6:00 ___	6:00 ___
6:30 ___	6:30 ___	6:30 ___	6:30 ___	6:30 ___	6:30 ___	6:30 ___
7:00 ___	7:00 ___	7:00 ___	7:00 ___	7:00 ___	7:00 ___	7:00 ___
7:30 ___	7:30 ___	7:30 ___	7:30 ___	7:30 ___	7:30 ___	7:30 ___
8:00 ___	8:00 ___	8:00 ___	8:00 ___	8:00 ___	8:00 ___	8:00 ___
8:30 ___	8:30 ___	8:30 ___	8:30 ___	8:30 ___	8:30 ___	8:30 ___
9:00 ___	9:00 ___	9:00 ___	9:00 ___	9:00 ___	9:00 ___	9:00 ___
9:30 ___	9:30 ___	9:30 ___	9:30 ___	9:30 ___	9:30 ___	9:30 ___
10:00 ___	10:00 ___	10:00 ___	10:00 ___	10:00 ___	10:00 ___	10:00 ___

From *Homework Improvement* published by GoodYearBooks. Copyright © 1996 Roberta Schneiderman with Stephen Werby.

Read It and Own It

Before Reading

Book _____ Chapter _____ Pages _____

I skimmed the ☐ Title   ☐ Heading   ☐ Subheadings

☐ Graphics   ☐ Highlighted Vocabulary   ☐ Questions

I think I will be reading about _____
_____
_____

☐ I need to read slowly to understand this material

☐ I know a lot about this material, so I will read more quickly

During Reading

Section Heading _____

Section Question _____

Facts to answer the question: _____ Number of facts

____ _____
____ _____
____ _____
____ _____
____ _____
____ _____

Vocabulary words to learn: _____
_____
_____

Read It and Own It

During Reading, continued

Section Heading _____

Section Question _____

Facts to answer the question: _____ Number of facts

___ _____

___ _____

___ _____

___ _____

___ _____

___ _____

___ _____

Vocabulary words to learn: _____

_____

_____

After Reading

I need to:

☐ Remember the information

    ___ I quizzed myself on the questions and facts and practiced in writing until I earned 100%.

    ___ I chose a method to study the vocabulary and practiced until I earned 100%.

☐ Discuss the material

    ___ I need to bring my Read It and Own It notes to school.

☐ Write about the material

    ___ I have specific directions about what I need to write about.

    ___ I need to get specific directions about what I need to write about.

Story Analyzer

Title _____

Author _____

Chapter/Pages _____

Names of characters (in this chapter) _____
_____
_____
_____

Settings (where and when the chapter took place) _____
_____
_____

What happened (briefly) _____
_____
_____
_____
_____
_____
_____
_____
_____
_____

Story Analyzer
Character Facts

Name of the character _____

Facts about the character   _____ Number of facts about the character

Flash Cards

Matching Deck

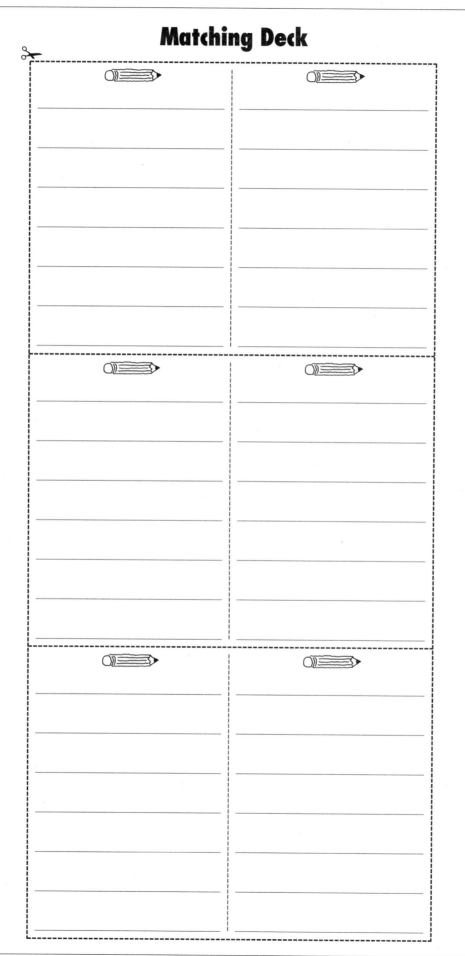

Sorting Box

Unknown

Sorting Box

1. Cut
2. Fold on dotted lines
3. Cut slot as shown
4. Fold in side flaps
5. Insert tab into slot
6. Tape as necessary

Sorting Box

Known

Sorting Box

1. Cut
2. Fold on dotted lines
3. Cut slot as shown
4. Fold in side flaps
5. Insert tab into slot
6. Tape as necessary

Split Sheet

Word	Association

Four-Column Page

Puzzle Chart

Writing Organizer

Topic Assigned _____

_____

Step 1. Discovery (Check each step as it is completed.)

___ I have thought about my topic.

___ I discussed my topic with another person.

___ I did some reading about my topic.

___ I made some notes about ideas that were uncovered during Discovery.

Step 2. Talking on Paper (Check each step as it is completed.)

___ I found a comfortable place to write.

___ I wrote for at least 15 minutes.

___ I wrote whatever came into my mind.

___ I ignored spelling, grammar, and sentence structure.

Step 3. Private Talking Out Loud (Check each step as it is completed.)

___ I read my words out loud to hear how they sounded.

___ I made some changes of things that didn't sound right.

Step 4. Public Talking Out Loud (Check each step as it is completed.)

___ I asked at least one person to listen to my paper as I read it.

___ I asked more than one person to listen to my paper as I read it.

___ I learned how people felt about what I read.

___ I did more thinking about my paper when people asked me questions.

Step 5. Cleaning (Check each step as it is completed.)

___ I went back to my comfortable writing spot.

___ I reread my paper and made changes.

___ I need to read my paper aloud to someone again; it still needs cleaning.

___ I have finished cleaning.

___ I like what I have written.

Step 6. Polishing (Check each step as it is completed.)

___ I checked my spelling.

___ I checked my sentences.

___ I checked my grammar.

___ I think my paper is polished.

Library Paper Builder

Assignment _____

_____

Step 1. Choosing My Topic (Check each step as it is completed.)

___ I have read much about my topic from _____ sources.
(specify the number)

___ I have thought a great deal about my topic.

___ I have discussed my topic with someone at home.

___ I have discussed my topic with my teacher.

___ I have made my topic very specific.

___ I can find enough information about my topic for the requirements.

___ I received approval for my topic from the teacher.

Step 2. Gathering (Check each step as it is completed.)

___ I am following the teacher's instructions for gathering my facts.

___ I did not have note-gathering instructions, and I am using note cards.

___ I have a separate group of cards for every source.

___ I have labeled the top note card of every group.

___ I have put each fact on a different note card.

___ I have labeled each note card with the page.

___ I have labeled each note card as a direct quote or a paraphrase.

___ I have briefly noted the source on each note card.

Step 3. Organizing (Check each step as it is completed.)

___ I read my notes aloud.

___ I listed all of my different ideas.

___ I arranged the different ideas into a logical order.

___ I placed my different ideas into an outline.

___ I placed my different ideas in order on one list.

___ I arranged my note cards to match the order of my outline or list.

Step 4. Talking on Paper (Check each step as it is completed.)

___ I found a comfortable place to write.

___ I followed my list or outline as I wrote.

___ I used my notes to find the facts as I wrote.

___ I put each new idea into a new paragraph.

Library Paper Builder, continued

Step 5. Private Talking Out Loud (Check each step as it is completed.)

___ I read my paper aloud to hear how it sounded.

___ I changed the things that didn't sound right.

Step 6. Public Talking Out Loud (Check each step as it is completed.)

___ I asked at least one person to listen to my paper as I read it.

___ I asked more than one person to listen to my paper as I read it.

___ I learned how people felt about what I read.

___ I did more thinking about my paper when people asked me questions.

Step 7. Cleaning (Check each step as it is completed.)

___ I went back to my comfortable writing spot.

___ I reread my paper and made changes.

___ I went back to my original sources to get more information to explain a confusing part.

___ I need to read my paper aloud to someone again; it still needs cleaning.

___ I have finished cleaning.

___ I like what I have written.

Step 8. Polishing (Check each step as it is completed.)

___ I checked my spelling.

___ I checked my sentences.

___ I checked my grammar.

___ I checked that I met all the requirements of the paper.

___ I think my paper is polished.

Problem and Reason Analyzer

Problem _____
_____

Reasons _____
_____
_____
_____
_____

Reason 1 _____

Whys _____
_____
_____
_____
_____

Possible Solutions _____
_____
_____

Test Analysis Form

Course _____

☐ Test
☐ Quiz
☐ Grade

Analysis of Errors

___ Forgot to Study
___ Did Not Understand
___ Careless Mistake
___ Panic
___ Memory Loss

Test Analysis Form

Course _____

☐ Test
☐ Quiz
☐ Grade

Analysis of Errors

___ Forgot to Study
___ Did Not Understand
___ Careless Mistake
___ Panic
___ Memory Loss

Test Analysis Form

Course _____

☐ Test
☐ Quiz
☐ Grade

Analysis of Errors

___ Forgot to Study
___ Did Not Understand
___ Careless Mistake
___ Panic
___ Memory Loss

Test Analysis Form

Course _____

☐ Test
☐ Quiz
☐ Grade

Analysis of Errors

___ Forgot to Study
___ Did Not Understand
___ Careless Mistake
___ Panic
___ Memory Loss

Footnotes

1. Greene, Georgeanne and Sally Habana-Hafner. *A Handbook on Home-School Collaboration* (Quincy, MA: Office of Community Education, Massachusetts Department of Education, 1988), p. 19, ERIC, ED 308 376.

2. Ibid., p. 1.

3. Cross, Christopher T. "Parental Involvement in Education." *Issues in Education.* (Washington, D.C.: Office of Educational Research and Improvement, August, 1990), p. 3. ERIC, ED 324 139.

4. Ibid., p. 2.

5. Ibid., p. 3

6. Piele, Philip K. (preface). *Involving Parents in the Education of Their Children,* by Thomas E. Hart (Eugene, OR: Oregon School Study Council, November, 1988), p. iii, ERIC, ED 300 930.

7. Ziegler, Suzanne. *The Effects of Parent Involvement on Children's Achievement: The Significance of Home/School Links* (Toronto, Ontario: Toronto Board of Education, October, 1987), p. 8, ERIC, ED 304 234.

8. Ibid., p. 9.

9. Ibid., p. 1.

10. Ibid., p. 4.

11. Ibid., p. 6.

12 U.S. Department of Education. *Strong Families, Strong Schools: Building Community Partnerships for Learning.* (Washington, D.C., September, 1994), p. 43.